THE LIBRARY
ST. MARY'S COLLEGE OF MARYLAND
ST. MARY'S CITY, MARYLAND 20686

AVIAN BIOLOGY
Volume VII

CONTRIBUTORS

Jacques Balthazart
Bruce Glick
Robert L. Rausch
Robert E. Ricklefs
Susan M. Smith
Glenn E. Walsberg

AVIAN BIOLOGY
Volume VII

EDITED BY

DONALD S. FARNER
Department of Zoology
University of Washington
Seattle, Washington

JAMES R. KING
Department of Zoology
Washington State University
Pullman, Washington

KENNETH C. PARKES
Carnegie Museum of Natural History
Pittsburgh, Pennsylvania

 1983

ACADEMIC PRESS
A Subsidiary of Harcourt Brace Jovanovich, Publishers
New York   London
Paris   San Diego   San Francisco   São Paulo   Syndey   Tokyo   Toronto

COPYRIGHT © 1983, BY ACADEMIC PRESS, INC.
ALL RIGHTS RESERVED.
NO PART OF THIS PUBLICATION MAY BE REPRODUCED OR
TRANSMITTED IN ANY FORM OR BY ANY MEANS, ELECTRONIC
OR MECHANICAL, INCLUDING PHOTOCOPY, RECORDING, OR ANY
INFORMATION STORAGE AND RETRIEVAL SYSTEM, WITHOUT
PERMISSION IN WRITING FROM THE PUBLISHER.

ACADEMIC PRESS, INC.
111 Fifth Avenue, New York, New York 10003

United Kingdom Edition published by
ACADEMIC PRESS, INC. (LONDON) LTD.
24/28 Oval Road, London NW1 7DX

Library of Congress Cataloging in Publication Data

Main entry under title:

Avian biology.

   Includes bibliographies.
   1. Ornithology. I. Farner, Donald Stanley,
Date   ed. II. King, James Roger, Date   ed.
[DNLM: 1. Birds. QL673 F235a]
QL673.A9   598   79-178216
ISBN 0-12-249407-5 (v. 7)

PRINTED IN THE UNITED STATES OF AMERICA

83 84 85 86   9 8 7 6 5 4 3 2 1

These volumes are dedicated to the memory of
A. J. "JOCK" MARSHALL
(1911–1967)

whose journey among men was too short by half

CONTENTS

CONTRIBUTORS	xi
GENERAL PREFACE	xiii
PREFACE TO VOLUME VII	xvii
NOTE ON TAXONOMY	xix
CONTENTS OF OTHER VOLUMES	xxiii

Chapter 1.   Avian Postnatal Development

Robert E. Ricklefs

I.	Introduction	2
II.	General Patterns of Development	4
III.	Developmental Change	12
IV.	Energetic and Nutritional Aspects of Growth	23
V.	Mathematical Description of Growth	30
VI.	Genetics of Growth	43
VII.	Susceptibility of Growth to Environmental Factors	51
VIII.	Intraspecific Variation in Postnatal Growth	58
IX.	Variation among Species	63
	References	72

Chapter 2.   The Ontogeny of Avian Behavior

Susan M. Smith

I.	Introduction	85
II.	Behavior of Embryos: Prehatching Behavior	90
III.	Behavior at Hatching	99
IV.	Posthatching Behavior	103
V.	Concluding Remarks	144
	References	145

Chapter 3.   Avian Ecological Energetics
Glenn E. Walsberg

I.	Introduction	161
II.	Energetics of Some Prominent Activities and Events in the Avian Life Cycle	164
III.	Total Energy Expenditure of Free-Living Birds	191
IV.	Concluding Comments	211
	References	212

Chapter 4.   Hormonal Correlates of Behavior
Jacques Balthazart

I.	Introduction	221
II.	The Classical Approach	223
III.	Attempts toward a Synthesis	260
IV.	Measuring Hormones and Their Fate	288
V.	Brain Mechanisms	304
VI.	Conclusions	334
	References	335

Chapter 5.   The Biology of Avian Parasites: Helminths
Robert L. Rausch

I.	Introduction	367
II.	Characteristics of Helminths	371
III.	Occurrence of Helminths in Birds	374
IV.	Specificity of Helminths	406
V.	Acquisition of Helminths by Birds	422
VI.	Localization of Helminths in the Avian Host	429
VII.	Pathogenicity of Helminths in Birds	430
	References	432

Chapter 6.   Bursa of Fabricius
Bruce Glick

I.	Introduction	443
II.	Morphology of the Bursa	444
III.	Origin of Bursal Lymphocytes	455
IV.	Bursal Microenvironment	458
V.	Bursal Kinetics	460
VI.	The Bursa's Influence on Other Organs	465
VII.	Regulation of Immunoglobulin Synthesis	467
VIII.	Summary	481
	References	484

CONTENTS

Author Index 501
Index to Bird Names... 523
Subject Index... 537

CONTRIBUTORS

Numbers in parentheses indicate the pages on which the authors' contributions begin.

JACQUES BALTHAZART (221), Laboratoire de Biochimie Générale et Comparée, Université de Liège, B-4020 Liège, Belgium

BRUCE GLICK (443), Poultry Science Department, Mississippi State University, Mississippi Agricultural and Forestry Experiment Station, Mississippi State, Mississippi 39762

ROBERT L. RAUSCH (367), Division of Animal Medicine and Department of Pathobiology, University of Washington, Seattle, Washington 98195

ROBERT E. RICKLEFS (1), Department of Biology, University of Pennsylvania, Philadelphia, Pennsylvania 19104

SUSAN M. SMITH (85), Department of Biological Sciences, Mount Holyoke College, South Hadley, Massachusetts 01075

GLENN E. WALSBERG (161), Department of Zoology, Arizona State University, Tempe, Arizona 85287

GENERAL PREFACE

The birds are the best known of the large and adaptively diversified classes of animals. About 8600 living species are currently recognized, and it is unlikely that more than a handful of additional species will be discovered. Knowledge of the distribution of living species, although much remains to be learned, is much more nearly complete than that for any other class of animals. Other aspects of avian biology may be less well known, but in general the knowledge in these areas surpasses that available for other animals. It is noteworthy that our relatively advanced knowledge of birds is attributable to a very substantial degree to a large group of dedicated and skilled amateur ornithologists.

Because of the abundance of empirical information on distribution, habitat, life cycles, breeding habits, etc., it has been relatively easier to use birds instead of other animals in the study of the general aspects of ethology, ecology, population biology, evolutionary biology, physiological ecology, and other fields of biology of contemporary interest. Model systems based on birds have had a prominent role in the development of these fields. The function of this multivolume treatise in relation to the place of birds in biological science is therefore envisioned as twofold: to present a reasonable assessment of selected aspects of avian biology for those having this field as their primary interest, and to contribute to the broader fields of biology in which investigations using birds are of substantial significance.

More than two decades have passed since the publication of A. J. Marshall's "Biology and Comparative Physiology of Birds," but progress in the fields included in this treatise has made most of the older chapters obsolete. Avian biology has shared in the so-called information explosion. The number of serial publications devoted mainly to avian biology has increased by about 20% per decade since 1940, and the spiral has been amplified by the parallel increase in page production and by the spread of publication into ancillary journals. By 1964, there were about 215 exclusively ornithological journals and about 245 additional serials publishing appreciable amounts of information on avian biology.*

These data reflect only the quantitative acceleration in the output of information in recent time. The qualitative changes have been much more impressive. Avifaunas that were scarcely known except as lists of species a decade ago have become accessible to investigation because of improved transportation and facilities in many parts of the world. New instrumentation has allowed the development of new fields of study and has extended the scope of old ones. Obvious examples include the use of radar in visualizing migration, of telemetry in studying the physiology of flying birds, and of spectography in analyzing bird sounds. The development of mathematical modeling, for instance, in evolutionary biology and population ecology has supplied new perspectives for old problems and a new arena for the examination of empirical data. All of these developments—social, practical, and theoretical—have profoundly affected many aspects of avian biology in the last decade. It is now time for another inventory of information, hypotheses, and new questions.

Marshall's "Biology and Comparative Physiology of Birds" was the first treatise in the English language that regarded ornithology as consisting of more than anatomy, taxonomy, oology, and life history. This viewpoint was in part a product of the times; but it also reflected Marshall's own holistic philosophy and his understanding that "life history" had come to include the entire spectrum of physiological, demographic, and behavioral adaptation. This treatise is the direct descendant of Marshall's initiative. We have attempted to preserve the view that ornithology belongs to anyone who studies birds, whether it be on the level of molecules, individuals, or populations. To emphasize our intentions we have called the work "Avian Biology."

It has been proclaimed by various oracles that sciences based on taxonomic units (such as insects, birds, or mammals) are obsolete, and that the forefront of biology is process oriented rather than taxon oriented. This narrow vision of biology derives from an understandable but nevertheless myopic philosophy of reductionism and from the hyperspecialization that characterizes so much of science today. It fails to notice that lateral synthesis as well as vertical analysis are inseparable partners in the search for biological principles. Avian biologists of both stripes have together contributed a disproportionately large share of the information and thought that have produced contemporary principles in zoogeography, systematics, ethology, demography, comparative physiology, and other fields too numerous to mention. The record speaks for itself.

*Baldwin, P. A., and Oehlert, D. E. (1964), "Studies in Biological Literature and Communications. No. 4. The Status of Ornithological Literature." Biological Abstracts, Inc., Philadelphia.

In part, this progress results from the attributes of birds themselves. They are active and visible during the daytime; they have diversified into virtually all major habitats and modes of life; they are small enough to be studied in useful numbers but not so small that observation is difficult; and, not least, they are esthetically attractive. In short, they are relatively easy to study. For this reason we find in avian biology an alliance of specialists and generalists who regard birds as the best natural vehicle for the exploration of process and pattern in the biological realm. It is an alliance that seems still to be increasing in vigor and scope.

In the early planning stages of the treatise we established certain working rules that we have been able to follow with rather uneven success:

1. "Avian Biology" is the conceptual descendant of Marshall's earlier treatise, but is more than simply a revision of it. We have deleted some topics and added or extended others. Conspicuous among the deletions are embryology and the central nervous system. Avian embryology, under a new banner of developmental biology, has expanded and specialized to the extent that a significant review of recent advances would be a treatise in itself. The avian brain has been treated very extensively in "The Avian Brain" by Ronald Pearson (Academic Press, 1972).

2. Since we expect the volumes to be useful for reference purposes as well as for the instruction of advanced students, we have asked authors to summarize established facts and principles as well as to review recent advances.

3. We have attempted to arrange a balanced account of avian biology as it stands at the 1970s–1980s. We have not only retained chapters outlining modern concepts of structure and function in birds, as is traditional, but have also encouraged contributions representing multidisciplinary approaches and synthesis of new points of view.

4. We have attempted to avoid a parochial view of avian biology by seeking diversity among authors with respect to nationality, age, and ornithological heritage.

5. As a corollary of the preceding point, we have not intentionally emphasized any single school of thought, nor have we sought to dictate the treatment given to controversial subjects. Our single concession to conceptual conformity is in taxonomic usage, as explained by Kenneth Parkes in the Note on Taxonomy.

We began our work with a careful plan for a logical topical development throughout all volumes. Only its dim vestiges remain. Owing to belated defections by a few authors and conflicting commitments by others we have been obliged to sacrifice logical sequence in order to retain authors whom we regarded as the best for the task. In short, we gave first priority to the maintenance of general quality, trusting that each reader would supply logical cohesion by selecting chapters that are germane to his individual interests.

DONALD S. FARNER
JAMES R. KING

PREFACE TO VOLUME VII

It is more than 15 years since we first sketched our plans for "Avian Biology." Subsequently, fields of inquiry that were only embryonic then have matured to a stage in which synthesis and review are now timely. The chapters by Balthazart and by Walsberg in Volume VII reflect this development. The other subjects in this volume were brought together either by our belated realization that they were indispensable in a treatise called "Avian Biology" or by our insistence on waiting until we could secure contributions from authentic experts on subjects previously omitted. This has resulted in a mélange of topics in Volume VII and a departure, more prominent here than in previous volumes, from our original plan for a steady thematic development through the series. We regard this compromise as the best of the alternatives, as it preserves our key working rule: expert and thorough treatment of every topic.

DONALD S. FARNER
JAMES R. KING
KENNETH C. PARKES

NOTE ON TAXONOMY

Early in the planning stages of "Avian Biology" it became apparent to the editors that it would be desirable to have the manuscript read by a taxonomist, whose responsibility it would be to monitor uniformity of usage in classification and nomenclature. Other multiauthored compendia have been criticized by reviewers for use of obsolete scientific names and for lack of concordance from chapter to chapter. As neither of the other editors is a taxonomist, they invited me to perform this service.

A brief discussion of the ground rules that we have tried to follow is in order. Insofar as possible, the classification of birds down to the family level follows that presented by Dr. Storer in Chapter 1, Volume I.

Within each chapter, the first mention of a species of wild bird includes both the scientific name and an English name, or the scientific name alone. If the same species is mentioned by English name later in the same chapter, the scientific name is usually omitted. Scientific names are also usually omitted for domesticated or laboratory birds. The reader may make the assumption throughout the treatise that, unless otherwise indicated, the following statements apply:

1. "Duck" or "domestic duck" refers to domesticated forms of *Anas platyrhynchos*.
2. "Goose" or "domestic goose" refers to domesticated forms of *Anser anser*.
3. "Pigeon" or "domesticated pigeon" or "homing pigeon" refers to domesticated forms of *Columba livia*.
4. "Turkey" or "domestic turkey" refers to domesticated forms of *Meleagris gallopavo*.
5. "Chicken" or "domestic fowl" refers to domesticated forms of *Gallus gallus*; these are often collectively called "*Gallus domesticus*" in biological literature.

6. "Japanese Quail" refers to laboratory strains of the genus *Coturnix*, the exact taxonomic status of which is uncertain. See Moreau and Wayre, *Ardea* **56,** 209–227, 1968.
7. "Canary" or "domesticated canary" refers to domesticated forms of *Serinus canaria*.
8. "Guinea Fowl" or "Guinea Hen" refers to domesticated forms of *Numida meleagris*.
9. "Ring Dove" refers to domesticated and laboratory strains of the genus *Streptopelia*, often and incorrectly given specific status as *S. "risoria."* Now thought to have descended from the African Collared Dove (*S. roseogrisea*), the Ring Dove of today *may* possibly be derived in part from *S. decaocto* of Eurasia; at the time of publication of Volume 3 of Peters's "Check-List of Birds of the World" (p. 92, 1937), *S. decaocto* was thought to be the direct ancestor of *"risoria."* See Goodwin, "Pigeons and Doves of the World," p. 129, 1967.

As mentioned previously an effort has been made to achieve uniformity of usage of both scientific and English names. In general, the scientific names are those used by the Peters "Check-List"; exceptions include those orders and families covered in the earliest volumes for which more recent classifications have become widely accepted (principally Anatidae, Falconiformes, and Scolopacidae). For those families not yet covered by the Peters list, I have relied on several standard references. For the New World I have used principally Meyer de Schauensee's "The Species of Birds of South America and Their Distribution" (1966), supplemented by Eisenmann's "The Species of Middle American Birds" (*Trans. Linn. Soc. N.Y.* **7.** 1955). For Eurasia I have used principally Vaurie's "The Birds of the Palaearctic Fauna" (1959, 1965) and Ripley's "A Synopsis of the Birds of India and Pakistan" (1961). There is so much disagreement as to classification and nomenclature in recent checklists and handbooks of African birds that I have sometimes had to use my best judgment and to make an arbitrary choice. For names of birds confined to Australia, New Zealand, and other areas not covered by the references just cited, I have been guided by recent regional checklists and by general usage in recent literature. English names have been standardized in the same way, using many of the same reference works. In both the United States and Great Britain, the limited size of the avifauna has given rise to some rather provincial English names; I have added appropriate (and often previously used) adjectives to these. Thus *Sturnus vulgaris* is "European Starling," not simply "Starling"; *Cardinalis cardinalis* is "North American Cardinal," not simply "Cardinal"; and *Ardea cinerea* is "Gray Heron," not simply "Heron."

Reliance on a standard reference, in this case Peters, has meant that certain species appear under scientific names quite different from those used in most of the ornithological literature. For example, the Zebra Finch, widely used as a laboratory species, was long known as *Taeniopygia castanotis*. In Volume 14 of Peters's "Check-List" (pp. 357–358, 1968), *Taeniopygia* is considered a subgenus of *Poephila*, and *castanotis* a subspecies of *P. guttata*. Thus the species name of the Zebra Finch becomes *P. guttata*. In such cases, the more familiar name will usually be given parenthetically.

For the sake of consistency, scientific and English names used in Volume I will be used throughout "Avian Biology," even though these may differ from names used in standard reference works that would normally be followed, but which were published after the editing of Volume I had been completed.

Strict adherence to standard references also means that some birds will appear under scientific names that, for either taxonomic or nomenclatorial reasons, would *not* be those chosen by either the chapter author or the taxonomic editor. Similarly, the standardized English name may *not* be the one most familiar to the chapter author. As a taxonomist, I naturally hold some opinions that differ from those of the authors of the Peters list and the other reference works used. I feel strongly, however, that a general text such as "Avian Biology" should not be used as a vehicle for taxonomic or nomenclatorial innovation or for the furtherance of my personal opinions. I therefore apologize to those authors in whose chapters names have been altered for the sake of uniformity and offer as solace the fact that I have had my objectivity strained several times by having to use names that do not reflect my own taxonomic judgment.

Addendum

Since the publication of Volume I of "Avian Biology," neither the taxonomists nor the coiners of English names for birds have been idle. In spite of the original intent to keep the names of birds uniform throughout the treatise, extension beyond the initially planned five volumes has warranted some modification. I have brought a few scientific names and English names into accordance with current usage, especially with regard to those accepted by the American Ornithologists' Union Committee on Classification and Nomenclature for use in the sixth edition of the "Check-List of North American Birds."

Perceptive readers will notice that certain widely accepted changes in scientific names have *not* been made here. This is either because I regard the taxonomic or nomenclatural questions as still open (so that the names used in Volumes I–V may prove to be correct) or because the earlier name appears so frequently and is so widely accepted that it would be especially confusing to change at this point. I believe that none of these decisions, to

change or not to change, will be troublesome for most readers.
Changes made as of Volume VI include the following:

1. *Anas acuta* becomes Northern Pintail, not Pintail.
2. *Troglodytes troglodytes* becomes Winter Wren, not Wren or European Wren.
3. *Junco hyemalis* becomes Dark-eyed Junco; "Slate-colored Junco" and "Oregon Junco" may be used for those subspecies groups.
4. Northern Gannet becomes *Sula [Morus] bassana*, not *Morus bassanus*.
5. Great Egret becomes *Casmerodius albus*, not *Egretta alba*.
6. American Woodcock becomes *Scolopax [Philohela] minor*, not *Philohela minor*.
7. Caspian Tern becomes *Sterna caspia*, not *Hydroprogne caspia*.
8. Common Redpoll becomes *Carduelis flammea*, not *Acanthis flammea*.
9. Eurasian Linnet becomes *Carduelis cannabina*, not *Acanthis cannabina*.

Changes made as of Volume VII include the following:

1. Red Phalarope becomes *Phalaropus fulicaria*, not *P. fulicarius*.
2. The former species *Sterna albifrons* is divided into two: the Old World *S. albifrons* (Little Tern) and New World *S. antillarum* (Least Tern).
3. Dovekie becomes *Alle alle*, not *Plautus alle*.
4. Burrowing Owl becomes *Athene cunicularia*, not *Speotyto cunicularia*.
5. The woodpecker genus *Dendrocopos* is merged into *Picoides*.

KENNETH C. PARKES

CONTENTS OF OTHER VOLUMES

Volume I

Classification of Birds
Robert W. Storer

Origin and Evolution of Birds
Pierce Brodkorb

Systematics and Speciation in Birds
Robert K. Selander

Adaptive Radiation of Birds
Robert W. Storer

Patterns of Terrestrial Bird Communities
Robert MacArthur

Sea Bird Ecology and the Marine Environment
N. Philip Ashmole

Biology of Desert Birds
D. L. Serventy

Ecological Aspects of Periodic Reproduction
Klaus Immelmann

Population Dynamics
Lars von Haartman

Ecological Aspects of Reproduction
Martin L. Cody

Ecological Aspects of Behavior
Gordon Orians

AUTHOR INDEX—INDEX TO BIRD NAMES—SUBJECT INDEX

Volume II

The Integument of Birds
Peter Stettenheim

Patterns of Molting
Ralph S. Palmer

Mechanisms and Control of Molt
Robert B. Payne

The Blood-Vascular System of Birds
David R. Jones and Kjell Johansen

Respiratory Function in Birds
Robert C. Laswieski

Digestion and the Digestive System
Vinzenz Ziswiler and Donald S. Farner

The Nutrition of Birds
Hans Fisher

The Intermediary Metabolism of Birds
Robert L. Hazelwood

Osmoregulation and Excretion in Birds
Vaughan H. Shoemaker

AUTHOR INDEX—INDEX TO BIRD NAMES—SUBJECT INDEX

Volume III

Reproduction in Birds
B. Lofts and R. K. Murton

The Adenohypophysis
A. Tixier-Vidal and B. K. Follett

The Peripheral Endocrine Glands
Ivan Assenmacher

Neuroendocrinology in Birds
Hideshi Kobayashi and Masaru Wada

Avian Vision
Arnold J. Sillman

Chemoreception
Bernice M. Wenzel

Mechanoreception
J. Schwartzkopff

Behavior
Robert A. Hinde

AUTHOR INDEX—INDEX TO BIRD NAMES—SUBJECT INDEX

Volume IV

The Peripheral and Autonomic Nervous Systems
Terence Bennett

The Avian Pineal Organ
M. Menaker and A. Oksche

The Avian Skeletomuscular System
Walter J. Bock

Thermal and Caloric Relations of Birds
William A. Calder and James R. King

Physiology and Energetics of Flight
M. Berger and J. S. Hart

AUTHOR INDEX—INDEX TO BIRD NAMES—SUBJECT INDEX

Volume V

Mechanics of Flight
C. J. Pennycuick

Migration: Control and Metabolic Physiology
Peter Berthold

Migration: Orientation and Navigation
Stephen T. Emlen

Circadian and Circannual Rhythms in Birds
Eberhard Gwinner

Vocal Behavior in Birds
Fernando Nottebohm

Incubation
Rudolf Drent

Zoogeography
François Vuilleumier

AUTHOR INDEX—INDEX TO BIRD NAMES—SUBJECT INDEX—ERRATA TO VOLUME III

Volume VI

Avian Mating Systems
Lewis W. Oring

The Ecology and Evolution of Avian Migration Systems
Sidney A. Gauthreaux, Jr.

Social Organization in the Nonreproductive Season
H. Ronald Pulliam and George C. Millikan

The Uropygial Gland
Jürgen Jacob and Vincent Ziswiler

Stomach Oils
Jürgen Jacob

The Glycogen Body
Louis D. De Gennaro

Domestication in Birds
Roland Sossinka

Respiration and Control of Breathing
Peter Scheid

AUTHOR INDEX—INDEX TO BIRD NAMES—SUBJECT INDEX

Chapter 1

AVIAN POSTNATAL DEVELOPMENT

Robert E. Ricklefs

I.	Introduction	2
II.	General Patterns of Development	3
	A. Altricial and Precocial Development	3
	B. Correlated Attributes of the Precocial–Altricial Spectrum	5
	C. Origins of the Precocial–Altricial Spectrum	9
III.	Developmental Change	12
	A. Behavior and Parental Care	12
	B. Anatomical Changes	13
	C. Development of Homeothermy	17
	D. Development of Skeletal Muscles	21
	E. Hormones and Growth	22
IV.	Energetic and Nutritional Aspects of Growth	23
	A. Energetics of Postnatal Development	23
	B. Nutrition and Postnatal Development	27
V.	Mathematical Description of Growth	30
	A. Purpose of Description	30
	B. Types of Data	30
	C. Types of Analyses	31
	D. Curve Fitting	33
	E. Relative Growth	41
	F. Longitudinal Correlations	42
	G. Multivariate Analyses	42
VI.	Genetics of Growth	43
	A. Components of Phenotypic Variance	43
	B. The Estimation of Variance Components	45
	C. Response to Selection	49
	D. Genetic Covariance and Correlated Responses to Selection	50
VII.	Susceptibility of Growth to Environmental Factors	51
	A. Force-Feeding	52
	B. Intermittent Feeding	53
	C. Drastically Restricted Food or Nutrient Intake	54
	D. Chronic Food Deprivation	55
	E. Cold Exposure	56
VIII.	Intraspecific Variation in Postnatal Growth	58
	A. Locality, Year, and Season	58
	B. Weather and Food Supply	59
	C. Brood Size	60

	D. Egg Size	61
	E. Brood Effects	62
IX.	Variation among Species	63
	A. Patterns of Interspecific Variation	63
	B. Hypotheses Concerning Growth Rates	66
	References	72

I. Introduction

The transformation from egg to adult is fundamentally important to the study of avian biology. This has long been recognized by developmentalists and poultry scientists, but only recently by most avian biologists. Even so, poultry research has focused rather narrowly on factors related to production, and developmentalists have been concerned primarily with the remarkable transformations of early embryogenesis. In Marshall's (1960–1961) treatise of two decades ago, Ruth Bellairs's (1960) chapter, *Development of Birds*, ended at hatching, as if development in the egg and growth of the chick conveniently defined different realms of inquiry, the latter perhaps a postscript concerned with the enlargement of structures established much earlier.

This chapter is about growth after hatching. The problem for the chick is to traverse the developmental gulf between neonate and adult with a minimum of risk to itself and with efficient utilization of the care provided by its parents. The exact course of development depends to some degree upon the size and body proportions of the neonate and adult and the environment of the chick during its development. Because of the central role of the parent in modifying the environment of the chick, development and parental care are closely coupled. Hence the study of development cannot be isolated from the broader study of behavioral and ecological aspects of avian reproduction.

Interest in avian development was stimulated by the unfolding of the body plan during the early embryonic period which, among the higher vertebrates, could be observed most easily in the eggs of domestic fowl. Chicks similarly proved to be convenient subjects for experimental physiology, as the observations by Pembrey *et al.* (1895) on the metabolic response of chicks to different temperatures demonstrated.

Early studies of postnatal development in birds were mostly descriptive and often examined the growth of species in the wild (e.g., Bergtold, 1913; Stanwood, 1913; Sumner, 1929). Huxley's (1924, 1932) mathematical treatment of the relative growth of parts of organisms stimulated many analyses of the growth of organs, such as those of Latimer (1924, 1925a,b, 1927) on the domestic fowl and Kaufman (1927, 1930) on the pigeon. Several early workers were concerned with the regulation of growth processes (e.g., Schmalhausen, 1930). The Swiss zoologist Adolf Portmann (1935) proposed a theory, rooted in orthogenesis, concerning the parallel evolution of development pattern and the size and complexity of the brain. Portman's ideas influenced thinking about avian development for decades, especially in Europe.

Practical concern about animal breeding, and the formalization of the theory of quantitative genetics in the 1920s led to an interest in the genetics and evolution of growth processes (Lerner, 1937; Cock, 1966), reaffirmed by evolutionary biologists. Practical concerns also led to research on growth as a process of production by domestic animals, reaching its acme in Samuel Brody's (1945) classic, *Bioenergetics and Growth*.

Biologists interested in the functioning of birds in their natural environments came only recently to appreciate the complexity of postnatal development. S. Charles Kendeigh, beginning with Kendeigh and Baldwin (1928), introduced the currency of energy to the economics of the chick's give-and-take relationship with its environment. The most recent major step, that of making the connection between developmental processes and Darwinian fitness, was taken by David Lack (1968), when he placed postnatal growth and other life-history attributes in an evolutionary context.

The problem of postnatal development is now more or less fully appreciated by its students in all its complexity, subtlety, and promise for the future. This chapter is by one of those students, whose interest is the evolutionary interpretation of the tremendous diversity of growth rates and developmental pathways followed by chicks from hatching to adulthood. Although I have consciously tried not to succumb to my own biases and have deemphasized topics recently reviewed elsewhere, this chapter inevitably expresses my interests in evolutionary ecology, if not in subject matter then in its treatment. The chapter is divided into three major parts. The first (Sections II–V) describes what happens during development. The second (Sections VI–VIII) discusses genetic and environmental bases for variation within populations. The last (Section IX) provides interpretations for differences in postnatal growth observed between species.

Perhaps the single most striking feature of postnatal growth in birds is the dichotomy between precocial and altricial development, which provides a logical and convenient starting point for this chapter.

II. General Patterns of Development

A. ALTRICIAL AND PRECOCIAL DEVELOPMENT

1. *Criteria for Classification*

The condition and functional capabilities of the neonate range from total independence (megapodes) to complete dependence upon parental care (e.g., passerines). A variety of contrasting terms have been used to describe the extremes of this range, but *precocial* and *altricial* are the most widely adopted, largely following Nice's (1962) usage. Precocial derives from classical roots refering to early ripening or maturing and evokes an image of developed function—feeding, mobility, and homeothermy—in the neonate. Altricial derives from the dependence of the neonate on its parents for nutrition. An alternative classification of neonates into nidifugous (nest-leaving) and nidicolous (nest-sitting) chicks has been used widely in Europe but is limited by its being restricted to a criterion of mobility and will not be used here.

Nice (1962) subdivided the precocial–altricial classification into eight categories based on the following criteria, determined at the time of hatching: eyes (open or closed), down (present or absent), nourishment (self or parental), mobility (ambulatory or nest-bound, i.e., nidifugous or nidicolous), and parental attendance, including brooding, food showing, defense (absent or present). This spectrum of criteria is illustrated in Fig. 1. Precocial 2 and 3 are distinguished by whether the parent shows food to the young. Precocial 4 chicks (rails and grebes) are fed by their parents for a short time after hatching.

Some of Nice's distinctions are subtle and of unknown functional significance. For example, semiprecocial and semialtricial chicks are separated by their potential mobility. Gulls and terns (semiprecocials) are capable of walking at hatching but remain at the nest site, at least briefly. Most of the ground-nesting species become highly ambulatory shortly thereafter, although tree nesters such as the White Tern (*Gygis alba*) and Black Noddy (*Anous minutus*) remain at the nest site until first flight. Young herons and hawks (semialtricials) remain in their nests for safety, but may possess functional capabilities similar to semiprecocials shortly after hatching. Semialtricial 1 and 2 are distinguished by whether the eyes are open or closed, a difference that persists only briefly and is of unknown significance to the chick.

There are a few species whose unusual mixtures of altricial and precocial features do not place them conveniently in any category. The Hoatzin (*Opisthocomus hoazin*) hatches with very sparse down but is extremely mobile from an early age (Nice, 1962). The Bearded Bellbird (*Procnias averano*), unlike most other Passeriformes, hatches with a covering of thick down (Snow, 1970). Skutch (1976) has suggested that the purpose of the down is to camouflage the chick in its nest, but Snow's observation that the single nestling is not brooded beyond the fourth day after hatching suggests the possibility of a thermoregulatory role.

Regardless of occasional difficulties, Nice's classification emphasizes that neonatal condition varies principally on a single axis from independence to dependence and that many intermediate combinations of precocial and altri-

Condition		Down	Eyes	Mobility	Parental nourishment	Parental attendance	Examples
Precocial	1	○	○	○	○	○	Megapodes
	2	○	○	○	○	●	Ducks, shorebirds
	3	○	○	○	○	●	Quail, grouse
	4	○	○	○	◐	●	Grebes, rails
Semiprecocial		○	○	◐	●	●	Gulls, terns
Semialtricial	1	○	○	●	●	●	Herons, hawks
	2	○	●	●	●	●	Owls
Altricial		●	●	●	●	●	Passerines

FIG. 1. Summary of the characteristics of the grades of altricial (●) and precocial (○) development according to Nice's (1962) classification.

cial features exist. It is conceivable that Nice's eight-category scheme may eventually be replaced by a quantitative, metrical classification based on measurements of structure and function, and incorporating the course of development as well as the condition of the neonate. For the present, however, the precocial–altricial distinction provides a useful basis for discussing patterns of postnatal growth.

2. Taxonomic Distribution of Neonatal Condition

Nice (1962) thoroughly discussed the taxonomic occurrence of the categories of neonates, revealing a close correspondence between development type and classification. Among 27 taxonomic orders considered, 19 occupy a fairly uniform position on the precocial–altricial spectrum, suggesting that development type is evolutionarily inflexible or, alternatively, that attributes of ecology or adult morphology that determine development type are inflexible. The most varied orders are the Charadriiformes, which range from the semialtricial Crabplover (Dromadidae) to many precocial 2's (shorebirds, primarily), and the Gruiformes, which range from precocial 4 (Gruidae) to semialtricial 1 (Cariamidae). According to Nice (1962) the Alcidae is the only family split between development types: precocial 2 or 3 (murrelets) and semiprecocial (most others). In general, the pattern is one of evolutionary conservatism.

B. Correlated Attributes of the Precocial–Altricial Spectrum

1. Egg Characteristics

In general, the eggs and neonates of precocial species are relatively larger than those of altricial species (Rahn et al., 1975). Comparisons are difficult because relative egg size generally bears an inverse relationship to adult size and precocial species tend to be larger than altricials. Rahn et al. (1975) circumvented this problem by basing their comparisons on extrapolations of egg weight–adult weight regressions to a common adult weight of 100 g, which was within the range of all the taxonomic orders considered. Evaluated at this adult size, the altricial orders have uniformly small eggs (4–10% of adult weight). Egg size then increases progressively from semialtricial orders (11–14%) to semiprecocial and precocial orders (9–21%). I follow Carey et al. (1980) and Ricklefs et al. (1980a) in designating Procellariiformes and Sphenisciformes as semiprecocial rather than semialtricial.

Although most of the precocial groups have large eggs, Galliformes (9%, precocial) have relatively smaller eggs than do Falconiformes (14%, semialtricial). R. J. O'Connor (unpublished) has pointed out that variation in relative egg size is fully consistent only with the presence of down (large eggs) and its absence (small eggs). Other criteria for development type (mobility and parental feeding) are not consistently related to egg size. This suggests that selection for early thermoregulatory ability and selection for large egg size may go hand in hand, but the wide range of relative egg sizes among precocial species indicates the influence of other factors.

Eggs of precocial species have relatively larger yolks than those of altricial species (Nice, 1962). The yolks also contain higher levels of lipid and protein (Ricklefs, 1977a). Carey et al. (1980) summarized data on yolk size, presenting their findings as a percentage of egg contents (i.e., excluding shell). Grouped according to Nice's (1962) development types, the proportions of yolk are precocial 1 = 65%, 2 = 44%, 3 = 41%, 4 = 30%; semiprecocial = 33%, semialtricial 1,2 = 26%, and altricial = 24%. The proportions are not only roughly consistent with development type, but also indicate a biologically important discontinuity between self-feeding precocials (2,3) and the more dependent precocial 4's and semiprecocials. How the relative size and quality of the yolk of the fresh egg are related to the condition of the neonate and the amount of its yolk reserve have not been adequately determined owing to a lack of data for most groups (see Ricklefs 1977a; Ricklefs et al., 1978; Williams et al., 1982).

2. Characteristics of the Neonate

One would expect the different functional attributes of precocial and altricial birds to be reflected in the body proportions of the newly hatched chick. On the basis of samples of four precocial species and four altricial species, Portmann (1950) demonstrated that neonates of the former group had relatively larger brains (4.2–7.2% versus 2.9–3.6%) and smaller intestines (6.5–10.5% versus 10.3–14.5%). These differences paralleled the greater activity and coordination of the precocial neonate and the greater preoccupation of altricials with eating and growing. When other components are considered, the differences between the neonates of altricial and precocial species become less consistent (see Table I). Precocials generally have relatively heavier integuments (skin plus feathers) and legs at hatching, which is consistent with their earlier development of homeothermy and pedal mobility, but they tend to have smaller pectoral muscles.

It is probably more meaningful to compare the body proportions of neonates relative to those of adults. If neonates with relatively large legs, for example, grow to be adults with relatively large legs, their proportions may more closely reflect adult form than the needs of chicks during early development. Portmann (1938) suggested that body proportions change during development to a greater degree in altricial species than in precocials. This appears to be true for the brain, which in precocials tends to be relatively large at hatching (Portmann, 1950) but small in adulthood (Sutter, 1943). Allometric constants (k) for other organs and body components, presented in Table II, reveal a different pattern. Organs with constants close to 1 maintain similar proportions throughout development (isomorphic growth). These in-

TABLE I

RELATIVE PROPORTIONS OF COMPONENTS OF ALTRICIAL AND PRECOCIAL NEONATES[a]

Component	Precocials[b]	Altricials[c]
Integument	13.5–17.6	9.0–13.3
Wings	1.3–3.7	2.6–4.3
Pectoral muscle	1.2–1.7	1.6–2.4
Legs	11.7–23.2	7.8–10.9
Head	16.0–20.0	14.5–26.2
Heart	1.3–1.5	0.7–1.6
Liver	2.6–5.4	2.7–3.6
Stomach	4.3–7.3	2.3–11.3

[a]Values in table are percentages of lipid-free weight of neonates; based on Austin and Ricklefs (1977), Ricklefs (1979a), Ricklefs et al. (1980a), and R. E. Ricklefs, W. A. Montevecchi, and D. Gabaldon (unpublished).

[b]Japanese Quail, Mallard, Leach's Storm-Petrel, and Common Tern.

[c]Rufous-winged Sparrow, European Starling, Mourning Dove, and Northern Gannet (*Sula bassana*).

clude the heart and liver for both altricials and precocials, the integument for precocials and perhaps altricials, and the legs for altricials. Where growth is heterogonous ($k < 1$ or $k > 1$), precocials generally have the more extreme values. This is particularly noticeable for the flight apparatus ($k > 1$) and legs ($k < 1$). For both development types, values of k for the head and stomach are considerably less than 1. From limited data I conclude, contrary to Portmann, that postnatal growth is less isomorphic in precocials than in altricials.

If the functional differences between altricial and precocial neonates are not evident in their body proportions, they should be reflected in the relative functional maturity of the tissues. A simple and convenient index to

TABLE II

ALLOMETRIC RELATIONSHIPS BETWEEN THE RELATIVE SIZES OF ORGANS IN NEONATES AND ADULTS ACCORDING TO DEVELOPMENTAL TYPE[a]

Component	Precocials[b]	Altricials[c]
Integument	0.87–1.24	1.06–1.14
Wings[d]	1.26–1.55	1.20–1.31
Pectoral muscles[d]	1.83–2.42	1.79–1.92
Legs[d]	0.38–0.97	0.93–1.06
Head	0.43–0.79	0.52–0.80
Heart	0.94–1.08	0.97–1.25
Liver	0.83–1.14	0.92–1.11
Stomach	0.69–0.85	0.55–1.01

[a]Allometric constraints (k) were calculated by the expression

$$k = \frac{(\log CM_A - \log CM_N)}{(\log BM_A - \log BM_N)}$$

where CM and BM designate component mass and body mass and subscripts A and N denote adult and neonate; based on Austin and Ricklefs (1977), Ricklefs et al. (1980a), R. E. Ricklefs, W. A. Montevecchi, and D. Gabaldon (unpublished), Latimer (1925a).

[b]Domestic Fowl, Japanese Quail, Leach's Storm-Petrel, and Common Tern (i.e., including semiprecocial species).

[c]Rufous-winged Sparrow, European Starling, Mourning Dove, and Northern Gannet.

[d]Data for domestic fowl not available.

maturity of a particular organ is its water content. In all tissues the percentage of water decreases throughout development (Bilby and Widdowson, 1971; O'Connor, 1977; Ricklefs, 1967b, 1975, 1979a), presumably as the proteins responsible for mature function accumulate. In neonates as a whole, water content is 78–82% in precocials and 84–86% in altricials. These consistent differences derive from those body components that function actively in precocials but not in altricials, such as the integument and legs (78–83% versus 83–88%). Components equally functional in both have similar ranges of water contents (e.g., heart 80–88% versus 82–89%, stomach 77–87% versus 79–84%), as do those that are equally undeveloped (e.g., pectoral muscles 82–86% versus 83–89%).

Placement of species in only two contrasting categories is necessary because so few comparative data are available. The distinction made by putting the division between semiprecocial and semialtricial development types is based primarily on thermoregulatory ability rather than nutrition and mobility. Indeed, the generation of heat may be as demanding upon the development of skeletal muscles as is locomotion and, in a developmental sense, may be the lowest common denominator of the precocial condition. We are nonetheless likely to discover as much variation within the two major development types as there are differences between them.

C. Origins of the Precocial–Altricial Spectrum

1. Portmann's Grades of Evolution

Adolf Portmann (1938, 1955) envisioned the progressive evolution of development type from primitive (megapodes) to advanced (passerines) accompanied by parallel trends in ontogeny and brain size: "*On peut conclure de ces faits qu'à coté de l'évolution de la forme adulte s'est effectuée une évolution des formes de l'ontogenèse* [Portmann, 1950, p. 534]."

The most primitive of Portmann's evolutionary stages is the self-feeding chick whose development is independent of adults and tends to be isomorphic. The second stage is transitional and involves the tying of otherwise ambulatory chicks to a particular area where they are fed by their parents. Because the transition is merely a step toward the inevitable altricial condition, Portmann supposed that one would find relatively few examples of this type. Portmann suggested the ground-nesting species of Caprimulgidae, which are downy and mobile but are fed close to the nest. The third state is associated with nesting above ground and involves a loss of down and a prolonged period of dependence. According to Portmann, parental care freed body development to stray from isomorphic growth—mature function of precocials demanded that body proportions at hatching be similar to those of adults—although this proposition is not well supported.

Portmann's ideas were orthogenetic and are difficult to defend in the context of current evolutionary thinking. The precocial neonate is undoubtedly the primitive condition, if only because the immediate reptilian ancestors of birds are presumed to have been precocial. Although the altricial condition is derived, and may have been so independently in different orders of birds, it is not useful to regard any development type as primitive or advanced, or to view the altricial condition as the logical and inevitable endpoint of evolutionary progress. Development types may be regarded as phenotypes optimized with respect to the particular environmental conditions of the species and in approximate evolutionary equilibrium, that is, with no net directional selection. Although it is useful to adopt this position in order to interpret the adaptive significance of development patterns, there lies a danger in equating correlation between adaptation and environment to evolutionary stasis. The immediate ecological position of a species is as much determined by its adaptations as vice versa. Even during an orthogenetic sequence one would expect to find a strong relationship between adaptation and environment. The broad taxonomic uniformity of development type argues against the presence of many transitional species. If, however, the basic dichotomy between precocial and altricial is bounded by a valley of low fitness in the adaptive landscape, once the valley is crossed evolution may lead quickly and inexorably to extreme altricial condition.

2. Ecological Factors

A strong correlation between precocial development and feeding either on the ground or in shallow water was recognized before bird studies made the transition from lore to science. Nice (1962) summed it up nicely: "Most precocial birds subsist on food that can be procured by young birds—small invertebrates or, occasionally, seeds. Some precocials in Class 4, as grebes and loons, semiprecocials and many altricials live on food that must be captured with strength and skill, so growth, maturation and learning are necessary before the chick can feed itself. In general, precocials nest on the ground, and altricials in trees. [p. 19]"

Type of food appears to be the overriding factor in establishing the precocial–altricial spectrum. With little imagination, most problematic species can be fit into the scheme quite easily. Grebes and loons are fed by their parents for several weeks after hatching, but they are physiologically and anatomically precocial and follow their parents from the nest shortly after hatching. Although there are no relevant data, one presumes that by their early maturation these chicks either avoid risks of predation in a vulnerable nest or reduce the need for their parents to make time-consuming and energetically expensive trips between feeding areas and the nest. Gulls, terns, many alcids, and petrels are fed at the nest site but are precocial with respect to temperature regulation. I believe that this condition is made necessary by the great distances between feeding and breeding areas in these species. Altricial development would require continuous nest attendance by one parent to maintain the chick's body temperature; short feeding bouts are not possible because of the long distance to a meal. Early development of homeothermy, although energetically costly, frees both parents to feed (Ricklefs, 1979a; Ricklefs et al., 1980a). A variation on this pattern involves taking the young chicks to the feeding area, as in the murrelets.

3. Further Considerations

The correlation between food resource and development type raises two questions. First, why are some combinations of traits never observed, for example, a nidifugous chick without down? Second, what advantage does the altricial condition confer when parents feed the young?

Active chicks have high thermal conductances. The difficulties for a parent faced with having to provide warmth to a dispersed brood and the unfavorable consequences of body cooling for a chick probably favor adaptations to retain heat. Because a strong capacity to generate heat comes hand in hand with locomotion, insulation further facilitates early thermal independence. If exceptions to this pattern were to exist, one would expect to find them among large-bodied, tropical birds like the Hoatzin.

The circumstance of downy chicks fed by their parents is quite common and presumably derives from the requirement of early homeothermy under certain conditions. When nest sites are close to or within feeding areas, species tend to adopt altricial development. But one might conceive of passerines feeding chicks that follow their parents in coveys like quail or having precocial chicks confined to a nest until exploding out to escape predation. Although there may be costs to maintaining developed tissues compared to undifferentiated tissues, overall expenditures for growth and temperature regulation by a brood confined to a nest should be independent of the precocity of development. The overwhelming advantage to altricial development seems to be rapid growth. As a group, altricials grow three to four times more rapidly than precocials (Ricklefs, 1973, 1979b; Case, 1978), and the difference between them may depend directly upon the degree of differentiation of the tissues (Ricklefs, 1979b; Section IX,B,7). Although adoption of the altricial condition may increase vulnerability to predators and enhance the effects of exposure to bad weather, these are presumably more than compensated for by the brevity of the development period.

III. Developmental Change

A. Behavior and Parental Care

1. General Trends

A general trend during postnatal development is from greater to lesser dependence upon parental care, and finally to complete independence. Chick development and parental care are complementary in that the behavior of adults is adjusted to the needs of their offspring. The extent of postnatal parental care varies from none, as in the megapodes, to complete dependence throughout the entire growth period, as in many passerines and other altricials. In some species, such as the Pelecaniformes and many Larinae, chicks are cared for well after their physical growth is completed, suggesting that experience-related components of development are important to the survival of the chick (Burger, 1980) and perhaps its eventual recruitment into the population as a breeding adult (e.g., Crawford, 1980; Ollason and Dunnet, 1978).

Development is gradual, but the progress of the chick can be measured against certain landmarks that provide a useful comparison among species: hatching, acquisition of homeothermy, pedal locomotion and fledging, flight, and independence. Although these events frequently occur in the order listed, there is no hard and fast rule of precedence. Self-feeding may come before flight and complete thermal independence (e.g., Galliformes) or after it (e.g., Passeriformes). Altricials exhibit wide variation in the time of nest leaving, ranging from swallows and swifts, which have long nestling periods and fly well at fledging, to anis (*Crotophaga*), which may clamber from the nest after 8 days, by which time they have achieved only 40% of adult weight (Oniki and Ricklefs, 1981). Although major behavioral landmarks may not exhibit great consistency in their appearance, anatomical and functional development (e.g., brain function, tissue differentiation) may follow a more uniform course, with differences in behavioral development superimposed upon this course by differences in the relationships of species to their environment.

1. AVIAN POSTNATAL DEVELOPMENT

2. Nice's Phases of Growth

Following the early lead of Kuhlmann (1909), Nice (1943, 1962) divided the growth period into six phases based on behavior:

1. Postembryonic: begging response present; hearing, but no sight
2. Preliminary: beginning of "comfort" movements; eyes open, preening, yawning, standing
3. Transition: stretching, crouching, maturation of comfort movements
4. Locomotory: leaving the nest, may or may not feed itself
5. Socialization: aggression, flight, bathing
6. Juvenile: precocious sexual behavior, copulatory attempts

In the altricial Song Sparrow (*Melospiza melodia*), phase I occupies 0–4 days posthatching; phase II, 5–6 days; phase III, 7–9 days; phase IV, 10–16 days; phase V, 17–28 days, and phase VI, 29–90 days. According to Nice (1962), precocials go through phase I in the egg, phases II and III within 24 hours of hatching (although not in semiprecocials), and phases IV–V within a few days to several weeks, corresponding to the onset of flight. These phases of development are described for many species by Nice (1943, 1962), but that work has not led to a general theory of behavioral development and the topic has received limited, mostly descriptive, attention.

B. ANATOMICAL CHANGES

1. A Precocial–Altricial Comparison

Features of development closely related to the differences between precocial and altricial birds are illustrated in Fig. 2, in which the Japanese Quail (*Coturnix* sp.) and European Starling (*Sturnus vulgaris*) are contrasted. Growth and development are compared on a modified age scale in which the ages are adjusted so as to make the curves of increase in body weight coincide (Ricklefs, 1967a, 1979a). For species whose growth is described by the logistic equation, the growth index is 0 at 50% of final weight, -1 at 10%, and $+1$ at 90%. The index is used to compare development with respect to overall size, but preserve the relative temporal scale of events. The precocial Japanese Quail requires about four times as long as the altricial European Starling to complete its postnatal increase in body mass, although the species are of comparable size (Ricklefs, 1979a).

At hatching (growth index = -1.4), quail walk about and have about 30–40% of the thermoregulatory capacity of adults under mild cold stress; ability to fly appears between growth index 0 and $+1$. When body masses

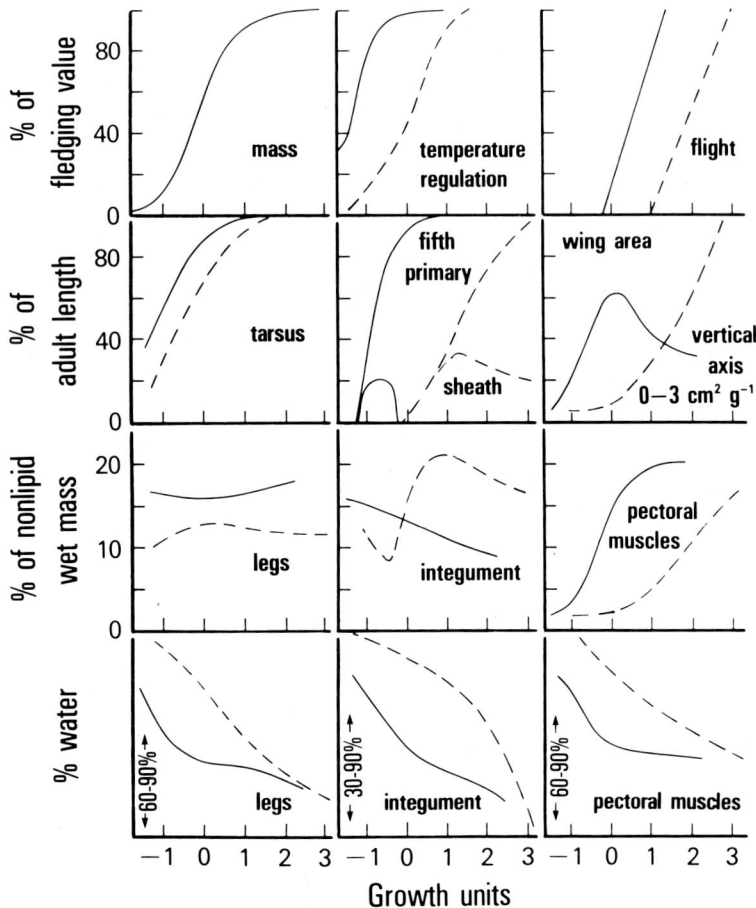

FIG. 2. A comparison of growth and development in a precocial bird (Japanese Quail; —) and an altricial bird (European Starling; ---). The ages are adjusted so that the curves of increase in body mass coincide (see text). (After Ricklefs, 1979a, and unpublished.)

are made to coincide, the growth of the quail and starling appear similar only in the length of the tarsus and relative size of the legs. In accordance with its precocial development, the quail exhibits anatomical traits consistent with mature function much earlier than the starling (e.g., decrease in the water content of tissues, increase in relative size of pectoral muscles, growth of feathers, and weight-specific area of the wing). There is also some indication in the quail of transitory conditions required to support mature function in a chick much smaller than adult size. For example, quail chicks begin to achieve level flight when the relative size and water content of the pectoral muscles approach adult values; but because the primaries are also almost full grown and because the chicks are only half of adult weight, their weight-specific wing area reaches a peak at the onset of flight that is considerably above the adult level. The greater wing area may help the younger chick to achieve lift, especially if its pectoral muscles cannot generate full power.

Anatomical aspects of growth vary with the development of function. Although semiprecocial species and many precocials acquire homeothermy and the ability to walk at an early age, they do not fly until almost full grown, and the development of their pectoral muscle and flight feathers is accordingly more like that of altricial birds (Ricklefs, 1979a). In the Leach's Storm-Petrel (*Oceanodroma leucorhoa*), however, the pectorals achieve relatively large size and low water content during the first 2 weeks after hatching, although chicks do not fly until 65–70 days. Apparently, the pectoral muscles provide much of the heat needed for thermoregulation at an early age (Ricklefs *et al.*, 1980a).

2. Studies of Proportional Change during Development

Although the data have not been adequately summarized or generalized, a large body of information on the growth of organs and other components of various species has accumulated. The most important papers are mentioned here. Earlier titles are either found in the American poultry literature or are European and largely were either written by Portmann's students or were stimulated by Portmann's work.

Latimer's (1924, 1925a,b, 1927) descriptions of the growth of the domestic fowl, although thorough, are long, tedious, and undigested. Kirkpatrick (1944) provided similar data for the Ring-necked Pheasant (*Phasianus colchicus*), as did Kaufman (1927, 1930, 1962) and Kaufman and Nowotna (1934) for the domestic pigeon, and Streich and Swetosarow (1937) for the domestic duck.

Portmann's students, among them Sutter, Schiess, and Neff, conducted more purposeful, usually comparative studies. Sutter (1943, 1951) described the growth of the brain in several precocial and altricial species, especially contrasting the brain of the European Quail (*Coturnix coturnix*) which is 6.3% of body weight at hatching but only 0.9% in the adult, with that of the European Starling (2.9 and 2.3%, respectively). Schiess (1963) compared the growth of extremities in waders (Charadriiformes). Neff (1972) conducted a thorough comparative study of the embryonic and postnatal growth of the viscera, brain, and eye in two precocial genera (*Anas* and *Gallus*) and six altricial genera (*Melopsittacus*, *Apus*, *Columba*, *Turdus*, *Passer*, and *Sturnus*).

More recently, a number of British and American studies have been directed toward interpreting interspecific variation in growth rate and development pattern. Anatomical details are provided by O'Connor (1977), Bryant and Gardiner (1979), Ricklefs 1967b, 1968a, 1975, 1979a), and Austin and Ricklefs (1977) for several passerines, by Ricklefs (1979a) for Japanese Quail and Common Terns (*Sterna hirundo*), Ricklefs and White (1981) for Common Terns and Sooty Terns (*Sterna fuscata*), Ricklefs et al. (1980a) for Leach's Storm-Petrel, and E. H. Dunn (1975b) for the Double-crested Cormorant (*Phalacrocorax auritus*).

3. Plumage Development

a. Downy Plumage of the Neonate. At hatching, the epidermal covering of altricial birds varies from naked (Pelecaniformes, Piciformes, Coraciiformes, some Passeriformes) through sparsely downy to very downy (e.g., bellbirds). Although most precocial neonates have dense downs, at least one species, the Hoatzin, is sparsely downy.

According to Fjeldså (1977) the structural relationships among the downy plumages of precocial birds are very complex and poorly understood. From an anatomical standpoint, the most primitive type of neonatal down is that of the grebes, in which the down does not have a separate quill but rather gradually merges into the feather as it grows. Down with a distinct shaft and lateral barbs is found in the waterfowl, megapodes, ratites, and tinamous. The more common situation, however, is a short shaft with a terminal spray of unhooked barbs. Numerous specializations described by Fjeldså are based on this type.

b. Replacement of the Down. In grebes, there is a continuum of downy barbs and hooked feather barbs on the same shaft, thus replacement occurs gradually as the feather grows and the tip wears off. In birds with distinctly differentiated down and feather quills, the down may be of two types: prepennae, in which the down is replaced by a feather growing from the same follicle, sometimes with an intervening "second generation" of down, and the preplumulae, in which the down is replaced by the juvenal down. Second generations of prepennae are found primarily in large, slowly growing birds such as the procellariiforms, pelecaniforms, cranes, and loons. In waterfowl, the second generation of down is plumulae, that is, the final underdown (Fjeldså, 1977). In the loons, the two generations of down (prepennae) develop from the same follicles as the feathers that replace them. In the Pelecaniformes, the down that develops posthatching consists of juvenal plumulae; there are no prepennae. In the Procellariiformes, there are two generations of prepennate down (Cramp, 1977). The situation is more complicated in many Falconiformes, in which the first down is prepennae and is succeeded by contour feathers; the "second" down, which is much thicker and soon overgrows the first, is the plumulae, or juvenal down (K. C. Parkes, personal communication). In the majority of birds, however, the juvenal plumage is preceded by a single generation of downs (prepennae) borne at the tips of the growing juvenal feathers.

Although the development of feathers has been described in great detail (Lucas and Stettenheim, 1972), few comparative analyses are available and the functional role of feathers during development is not well understood. One consequence of the loss of water as plumage and, to a lesser extent, other organs mature is a loss of mass by the nestling during the latter part of the development period (Ricklefs, 1968a). This phenomenon occurs in species such as swallows and swifts that have long prefledging periods relative to completion of growth in body mass. In these species, loss of water in the plumage occurs after the masses of other components have leveled off and therefore is expressed as a decrease in the total mass of the bird. Such decreases in many species, where mass recession ranged between 10 and 30% of adult weight, had previously been attributed to utilization of lipids during a prefledging phase of high energy demand, among other factors. Loss of mass by other species that accumulate large lipid deposits as nestlings, especially Procellariiformes, may involve metabolism of lipid as well, but there is no evidence bearing directly on this question.

Contour and flight feathers begin their growth at different times in development and grow at different rates in different species. There is some indication that rapidly growing feathers have a longer basal pulp (Ricklefs, 1979a; Fig. 2) and therefore, contain more water and are a potentially greater avenue of heat loss than are slowly growing feathers. But the functional significance and consequence of different patterns of feather growth are not well understood.

C. Development of Homeothermy

At hatching, chicks of altricial species do not respond metabolically to cold ambient temperatures and are unable to maintain their body temperatures above that of their surroundings. Precocial neonates generally exhibit marked thermogenic responses to cooling, but their homeothermic capacities vary greatly among species (e.g., Koskimies, 1962; Koskimies and Lahti, 1964). In all species, the level of thermoregulation increases during the development period. The earliest systematic studies on the acquisition of homeothermy were those of Pembrey (1895) and Pembrey et al. (1895). Subsequent studies by Kendeigh and Baldwin (1928), Baldwin and Kendeigh (1932), and Böni (1942) provided the foundation for modern work. Summarizing the literature, King and Farner (1961) cited the following factors as contributing to the development of homeothermy in young birds: (1) decrease in surface-to-volume ratio, (2) improvement of insulation, (3) increase in rate of thermogenesis, (4) possibly, the development and functioning of the air sacs, and (5) development of nervous and hormonal control, including the development of a central, presumably hypothalamic, temperature-sensitive regulatory center.

The development of temperature regulation has been reviewed by E. H. Dunn (1975a), Freeman (1971), O'Connor (1975a,c), Ricklefs (1974), and Shilov (1973). Shilov's book contains data not otherwise readily available on temperature change under cold stress, rates of oxygen consumption, blood chemistry, glycogen levels in liver, and evaporative water loss, mostly for passerines. Among Shilov's findings are that in small passerines levels of hemoglobin and blood sugar and numbers of erythrocytes about double between hatching and the onset of homeothermy, which is undoubtedly related to the increasing metabolism of the nestlings. In the same species, glycogen levels in the liver, serving as carbohydrate storage, reach a marked peak early in development and then fall by nearly two-thirds with the onset of homeothermy.

1. Surface-to-Volume Ratio

Because surface increases approximately as the two-thirds power of mass, the ratio of heat production (mass related) to heat loss (surface related) increases as the one-third power of mass. As a bird doubles its mass, its relative ability to produce and conserve heat increases about 1.26-fold, all other things being equal. Although age and relative size at onset of homeothermy vary greatly among species having the same body mass, increase in mass is nonetheless an important consideration. Nestlings of altricial birds become functionally homeothermic much earlier in large broods than in small broods or compared to individual chicks in metabolism chambers (Mertens, 1969; Yarbrough, 1970; O'Connor, 1975a; Dunn 1976, 1979b; Clark and Balda, 1981), demonstrating the contribution of mass to heat conservation. Moreover, chicks of larger species tend to acquire homeothermy at a lesser proportion of adult mass than do those of smaller species (E. H. Dunn, 1975a).

Balmer and Strobusch (1977) have suggested that considerations of surface area and heat loss place a lower limit on the size of precocial neonates. They argued that the effective surface area of the chick is the outer surface of the insulation which, if maintained at a constant thickness, does not decrease as

1. AVIAN POSTNATAL DEVELOPMENT

rapidly as the two-thirds power of mass. As the radius of the body core becomes small compared to the thickness of the down, the outer surface of the down decreases very slowly as mass decreases and the ratio of surface to mass increases rapidly. This problem can be circumvented only by reducing the thickness of the down, which also facilitates heat loss. Such considerations are a plausible explanation for the facts that the smallest precocial neonates are considerably larger than the smallest altricial neonates, and that the chicks of small precocial species have a prolonged development of homeothermy [e.g., the Painted Quail (*Coturnix chinensis*), neonate = 3 g, (Bernstein, 1973)].

2. Improvement of Insulation

The acquisition of homeothermy is clearly associated with the development of insulating plumage, although nestmates and the nest lining allow many altricials to develop significant temperature regulation in advance of a well-developed integument (Clark and Balda, 1981; Dunn, 1976, 1979b; Yarbrough, 1970). In spite of the central importance of insulation there have been few direct investigations of its contribution to the development of homeothermy.

Shilov (1973) compared the consumption of oxygen at 10 and 30°C by shaved and intact nestlings of the Great Tit (*Parus major*) and Pied Flycatcher (*Ficedula hypoleuca*). Shilov found that removing the feathers elevates oxygen consumption about 15% in the flycatcher and 25% in the tit after the onset of thermoregulation (9–10 days). The difference between nestlings with and without their normal insulation is surprisingly small. Spiers *et al.* (1974) investigated changes in the plumage of Japanese Quail chicks between hatching and 16 days, by which time chicks have approached adult levels of homeothermy. During this period, mass increased 6.0 times, surface area 3.8 times, and the ratio of plumage mass to surface area 4.4 times. However, McNabb and McNabb (1977a) found that the insulative capacity of small areas of integument, measured by physical means, increased by only 22% between 0 and 14 days. The permeability of the skin to water decreased 50%, thus reducing evaporative heat loss, but this constitutes a small part of the total heat budget of the chick.

3. Development of Air Sacs

Although the air sacs have been suggested as playing a possible role in the development of homeothermy, it is difficult to envision how they could enhance heat conservation except by minimal insulation of the body core when skin temperature is lowered. The air sacs are thought to aid heat dissipation by increasing surface area internally, especially during flight when oxygen demand is high and danger of alkalosis from hyperventilation is low (King, 1966; Salt, 1964).

4. Development of Thermogenesis

The generation of heat in response to cold stress is thought to be accomplished in birds solely by shivering of the skeletal muscles (West, 1965; Calder and King, 1974). Freeman (1971) and Wekstein and Zolman (1969) have presented evidence consistent with the existence of limited nonshivering thermogenesis in the domestic fowl during the first week after hatching, although it is clear that neonates also shiver.

Because the skeletal muscles are the primary seat of thermogenesis it is not surprising to find a close correlation between their growth and maturation and the acquisition of homeothermy. Leg muscles are a larger proportion of the chick during early development and, in some species, mature at an earlier age than the pectoral muscles (e.g., Ricklefs, 1975, 1979a). Hence the legs are probably the most important sources of heat during early stages of the development of temperature regulation. Aulie (1976a,b) stressed the importance of the growth and maturation of the pectoral muscles to the development of heat production in the Willow Ptarmigan (*Lapopus lagopus*). The leg muscles remain a rather constant proportion of body mass (3–4%) between hatching and 24 days; the pectoral muscles increase from less than 2% of body mass at hatching to about 12% by 2 weeks. Aulie also found that electrical potentials of pectoral muscles increased greatly during the first 3 days in response to cold stress, but did not change beyond that age, indicating the early maturation of function. I have already mentioned the unusual situation in storm-petrels whose pectoral muscles increase to a relatively large proportion of the chick's mass and appear to become functional well before the acquisition of flight, presumably as a source of heat for thermoregulation.

5. Development of Nervous and Hormonal Control

Panting has been observed well before the onset of thermogenesis in many species of altricial birds, indicating that a central temperature sensor is present and that it can stimulate motor activity (e.g., Kendeigh, 1939; Bartholomew, 1966; O'Connor, 1975d). Shivering appears at the same time as the earliest evidence of metabolic response to cooling in House Wrens (*Troglodytes aedon;* Kendeigh, 1939; Odum, 1942) and Mourning Doves (*Zenaida macroura;* Breitenbach and Baskett, 1967). It is unclear whether nerve development or muscle development determines the onset of thermogenesis, or if both are parallel expressions of the maturation of muscle.

Although histological and histochemical measures of the development of thyroid function have been temporally related to the acquisition of homeothermy (Dawson and Allen, 1960; McNabb and McNabb, 1977b), no direct connection with thermogenesis has been established.

D. Development of Skeletal Muscles

Changes in skeletal muscles are discussed in some detail here because of their major contribution to thermogenesis and to the distinctiveness of precocial and altricial chicks. In this sense, muscle serves as a useful model tissue for understanding variations in patterns of development more generally (Ricklefs, 1979b).

Changes in the muscles of the domestic fowl have been described by Csapo and Herrmann (1951), Herrmann (1952), Dickerson (1960), and King and King (1973). Enzymes involved in oxidative metabolism and contractile proteins increase in concentration according to the development of function by the muscle. As one would expect, posthatching changes are greater in the pectoral muscles than in those of the leg, which has achieved a greater level of function by the time of hatching. For example, between 0 and 63 days, the concentration of actin increases from 8 to 12 mg g^{-1} in the gastrocnemius muscle, but from 4 to 11 mg g^{-1}, mostly during the first 2 weeks, in the pectoralis (King and King, 1973). During the first $2\frac{1}{2}$ weeks after hatching in Rhode Island Red chicks, the sartorius muscle increases 2.2-fold whereas the pectorals increase 10.5-fold (Dickerson, 1960). During the same period, the water content of the pectoral muscles decreases from 85.4 to 77.1% as the concentration of protein about doubles. Adult levels of both fibrillar and sarcoplasmic proteins are attained by 2–4 weeks of age.

Aulie and Steen (1976) showed that increase in the weight of the pectoral muscles of Willow Ptarmigan chicks between hatching and 12 days occurs by growth of muscle fibers rather than by increase in their numbers. During that period, the weight of the muscle increased 32-fold, whereas fiber diameter increased 3.4-fold. Dividing 32 by 3.4^2, an index to the increase in cross-sectional area, results in 2.8, the factor by which Aulie and Steen suggested that fibers lengthened. Moss (1968a) investigated the weight, fiber cross-sectional area, and DNA content (an estimate of the number of nuclei) in pectoralis and gastrocnemius muscles of New Hampshire and White Leghorn chickens between 0 and 166 days. Moss suggested that fibers grow as new muscle cells produced by proliferating myoblasts fuse with them. This idea was based on the observation that the allometric relationships of DNA content and fiber cross-sectional area to weight of the pectoral muscles were nearly the same [0.66–0.70 versus 0.71–0.73, standard error (SE) = 0.04] in several replicated samples. Hence cross-sectional area and DNA content remained in direct proportion throughout development. Muscle fibers are formed initially by the fusion of the myoblasts to form a syncytium, after which the nuclei no longer divide. Apparently, fiber growth is supported by the continual incorporation of new myoblasts derived from a pool of proliferating cells.

E. Hormones and Growth

The role of hormones in avian growth has been reviewed in the course of more general discussions of endocrinology by Assenmacher (1973), Falconer (1971), Hartree and Cunningham (1971), Tixier-Vidal and Follett (1973), Sturkie (1976), and Meier and Ferrell (1978). Investigations have concentrated primarily on the effects of two substances, growth hormone (GH) and thyroid hormone.

Growth hormone isolated from the pituitary of the fowl exhibits an immunologic cross-reaction with that of the rat (Hayashida, 1969), indicating molecular homology, but not with that of the cow (Moudgal and Li, 1961). Chicken GH has been shown to stimulate growth of hypophysectomized rats in some studies (Hazelwood and Hazelwood, 1961; Moudgal and Li, 1961) but not others (Solomon and Greep, 1959). Although hypophysectomy of growing chickens retards growth (Nalbandov and Card, 1942; King, 1969), mammalian GH apparently has no stimulating effect on chicks (Libby *et al.*, 1955; Glick, 1960).

Disruption of thyroid activity by surgical thyroidectomy, radiothyroidectomy, or chemical inhibition of thyroid hormone has a severe retarding effect on growth (Blivaiss, 1947; Winchester and Davis, 1952; Marks, 1971; King and King, 1973; Howarth and Marks, 1973). Blivaiss (1947) found that thyroidectomy of the fowl at 6–10 days reduced eventual weight by 35% compared to controls, retarded bone and feather growth, and produced obesity. Voitkevich (1966) presented details of several experiments with thyroidectomy, which greatly retarded development if done at a young age. Ducklings operated on at 5 days weighed 800 g at 90 days versus 2500 g for controls. When operated on at 25 days (~600 g) growth slowed immediately and body weight increased only to 1100 g by 90 days. Thyroidectomized individuals were fat, but skeletal ossification and feather growth were retarded. The liver, adrenal glands, and kidneys, however, were four times larger than those of controls based on percentage of body weight.

Thyroid secretion levels are correlated with growth rate (Tanabe, 1965; Voitkevich, 1966) and development of homeothermy (Spiers *et al.*, 1974) but the manner of effect of thyroid hormone on development is not known. King and King (1973) measured the effects of severe hypothyroidism on development of leg muscles in the fowl after 4 weeks. Muscle mass was 0% (sartorius) and 20% (gastrocnemius) lower than in controls, but DNA levels were reduced 22 and 35%, suggesting a major effect on cell proliferation. According to Raheja and Snedecor (1970), decreased growth in thyroidectomized fowl is associated with decreased food intake, by about 25% in their study. Percentage assimilation of protein, fat, and energy was unaffected, but food intake per gram of mass gained increased by 5–10%.

Provision of exogenous thyroid hormone usually fully reverses the effects of thyroidectomy (Voitkevich, 1966; Raheja and Snedecor, 1970; King and King, 1973). Singh *et al.* (1968) demonstrated that providing supplementary thyroxine to intact chicks accelerated growth slightly when administered in moderate doses (2–4 µg 100 g^{-1} day^{-1}) and depressed growth slightly at higher doses (6 µg 100 g^{-1} day^{-1}). Normal thyroxine secretion levels decrease from about 2 µg 100 g^{-1} day^{-1} at 2 weeks to about 0.5 µg 100 g^{-1} day^{-1} at 100 days (Tanabe, 1965). In the experiment by Singh *et al.* (1968) the maximum effect was to increase growth rate by about 5% (i.e., 400–420% gain between 7 and 39 days).

Although the removal of GH and thyroid hormone have severe retarding effects, neither apparently is able to stimulate growth appreciably.

IV. Energetic and Nutritional Aspects of Growth

A. Energetics of Postnatal Development

Studies on the energy expenditures of growing chicks have been reviewed by Ricklefs (1974), O'Connor (1975c, 1978c), Kendeigh *et al.* (1977), Dunn (1980), and Drent and Daan (1980). Although some patterns of energy requirement are beginning to emerge, major questions about the adaptive significance of energetic considerations remain, and there is an increasing awareness that the nutritional balance of the diet may impose important restrictions on the rate and pattern of development. The general features of the energetics of chicks are summarized next.

The energy density (energy equivalent of tissues divided by fresh mass) generally increases with age owing to a decrease in level of water in the tissues and the accumulation of fat (Ricklefs, 1974). Energy densities of precocial neonates are generally greater than those of altricials because of lower water content and greater reserves of stored fat. The subsequent increase in energy density is generally greater in altricials than in precocials because the altricials undergo greater developmental change in body composition. However, many precocial and semiprecocial species store large quantities of lipids during their development, the procellariiforms being extreme examples, and their energy densities increase greatly as well.

The mass-specific basal metabolic rate (BMR) of chicks is generally low during the period immediately following hatching, rises, often quickly, then gradually drops to the adult level. In precocial birds, the first phase is often less pronounced than it is in altricials, and peak BMR is both earlier and higher (see Ricklefs, 1974).

The overall energy budget of the chick can be partitioned into growth, maintenance, temperature regulation, activity, and excretion and defecation, although in practice it is difficult to do so by direct measurement on chicks in natural environments. In most species, growth appears to be a relatively small part of the total energy expenditure, especially towards the later part of the development period when growth rate slows and the energy directed towards activity increases. Dunn (1980) estimated the energy expenditures for growth for several species of birds. Expressed as a percentage of the BMR of chicks, these values tended to decrease in a more or less linear fashion from hatching levels of about 250% for the Herring Gull (*Larus argentatus*) and Double-crested Cormorant, and 70% in the Pigeon Guillemot (*Cepphus columba*) and Dunlin (*Calidris alpina*) to 0% at the end of the growth period. These levels represent energetic growth efficiencies (growth energy divided by metabolized energy) at hatching of about 50% in the cormorant and gull, 40% in the guillemot, and less than 20% in the Dunlin. In other studies, energetic efficiencies during the early growth period have been estimated to be 31 and 46% in Common and Sooty terns (Ricklefs and White 1981), 56% in Leach's Storm-Petrel (Ricklefs *et al.*, 1980b), and 75% in House Martins (*Delichon urbica*; Bryant and Gardiner, 1979). The last value is on the order of the net efficiency of the growth of tissues (Ricklefs, 1974; Millward and Garlick, 1976).

Growth efficiency over the entire development period is difficult to estimate in many species because the end of the period is arbitrarily defined. Estimates for four species from hatching until first flight demonstrate the range of variation to be expected among species fed by their parents: House Martin 35–40%, Leach's Storm-Petrel 25% (not counting prefledging period of weight loss), Sooty Tern 24%, and Common Tern 21%. These estimates are probably high because energy expenditures for activity were not measured. Drent and Daan (1980) report a range of growth efficiencies from the literature of 22–29% for passerines, 25% for the Common Gull, and 19% for the Wood Stork.

Energetic growth efficiency is determined in large part by rate of growth and accumulation of fat, on one hand, and activity and expenditures for temperature regulation, on the other. Precocial birds ought to have much lower growth efficiencies than altricial birds because of their slow growth. The slower growth of the Sooty Tern in the tropics is offset by the higher costs of temperature regulation of the Common Tern in temperate regions, resulting in similar energetic efficiencies. The energetic efficiency of the slowly growing Leach's Storm-Petrel is relatively high because of lipid accumulation, which accounts for 87% of the energy in "growth" prior to prefledging mass loss during the last week of the nestling period.

Although growth may contribute a substantial portion of the total energy expenditure of the chick during the early part of the development period, it appears to have relatively little influence on expenditures during the latter part of the development period and, especially, the maximum energy requirement of the chick (Drent and Daan, 1980; Dunn, 1980; Ricklefs et al., 1980b; Ricklefs and White, 1981). An exception to this pattern was reported by Bryant and Gardiner (1979), who determined that the peak requirement of House Martins for growth occurred after other expenditures had leveled off and therefore resulted in a major peak in total expenditures. In other species, peak growth expenditures occur before the chicks are full grown, hence the sum of all expenditures exceeds by little, if any, that of maintenance, activity, and temperature regulation of the full-grown chick. This pattern of energy requirement has important consequences for any parent that feeds its young and whose fecundity is inversely related to the maximum requirements of its chicks, and it implies that large changes in growth rate would have a relatively small effect on maximum energy expenditure in such species.

That the energy expenditures of small chicks are far less than they become later in the development period suggests that chicks initially are not able to utilize fully the feeding capacities of their parents. It is not known whether this is due to limitation by the food processing apparatus, by the nutritional capacity of the diet to support growth, or by tissue level constraints on growth rate (Ricklefs, 1969a, 1979b). Some of these factors will be considered later (Section IX,B).

Fat deposition is an important component of the energy budgets of the chicks of many species of birds. Although some hatch with substantial reserves of yolk (Schmekel, 1961; summary in Ricklefs, 1974), yolk sacs are utilized early in development, particularly by precocial species that have difficulty feeding during the first few days after hatching. Fat needed as insurance against poor feeding conditions during the nestling period or as a reserve for the juvenile after independence from its parents must be accumulated during the development period. Fat levels generally increase during the growth period but there are marked differences between species. O'Connor (1978c) noted that aerial-feeding passerines deposited more fat as nestlings than did the chicks of other groups of species and suggested that the level of fat was adjusted to the irregularity of the food supply during the nestling period.

Lipid reserves are perhaps best measured relative to the rate of energy expenditures of the chicks; survival time in the absence of feeding should be approximately the ratio of the energy equivalent of lipid to the maintenance energy requirement. Ricklefs and White (1981) calculated these times as 2.9, 3.8, and 4.8 days for 5-, 20-, and 40-day-old Sooty Terns, and 0.4, 1.0, and 1.4 days for 2.5-, 10-, and 20-day-old Common Tern chicks. The large quantities of lipid stored by Leach's Storm-Petrel chicks predict minimal survival times of 3, 6, and 8 days for chicks aged 5, 20, and 40 days (based on Ricklefs et al., 1980b). These survival times are in accordance with the amount of lipid stored relative to the lipid-free dry weight of the chick, approximately 0.24 in the Common Tern (20 days), 0.35 in the Sooty Tern (40 days), and 1.5 in the storm-petrel (40 days). Comparable values reported for passerines are House Sparrow (*Passer domesticus*), 0.27; Blue Tit (*Parus caeruleus*), 0.35; and House Martin, 0.75 at fledging (O'Connor, 1978c); Cactus Wren (*Campylorhynchus brunneicapillus*) 0.1–0.3 (Ricklefs, 1975); Rufous-winged Sparrow (*Aimophila carpalis*), 0.1–0.2 (Austin and Ricklefs, 1977); Red-winged Blackbird (*Agelaius phoeniceus*), 0.1–0.2; and Barn Swallow (*Hirundo rustica*), 0.2–0.5 (Ricklefs, 1968a). These data are consistent with O'Connor's (1978c) predictions about the extent of fat depositon in nestlings relative to variability of the food supply. Fat also appears to be stored by some species in anticipation of greatly increased energy demands or sudden self-reliance for food after fledging, as in the gannets (*Sula* spp.; Nelson, 1966). Proper evaluation of these hypotheses will require more comparative information on trends in fat levels and variation about the trends relative to feeding conditions.

Perhaps the most unusual pattern of fat deposition is exhibited by the Procellariiformes, whose peak mass during the nestling period may be more than twice the adult mass. Although much of this mass is lost during a brief period before fledging, changes in lipid level during this period have not been measured directly. Lipid reserves are thought to supply energy during normal intervals between feeds or during long absences of adults caused by storms or poor feeding conditions (Lack, 1968). It is also possible that lipid storage, which amounts to 25% of the metabolizable energy between 0 and 60 days in Leach's Storm-Petrel, acts as an energy sink to accommodate the energy-rich diet and enable the chick to accumulate limiting nutrients (Ricklefs et al., 1980b). The Oilbird (*Steatornis caripensis*), a tropical caprimulgiform that feeds its chicks exclusively on oil-rich fruits, stores enormous quantities of lipid during the nestling period, much of which presumably is metabolized prior to fledging (Snow, 1960–1961; White, 1974).

B. Nutrition and Postnatal Development

The nutritional requirements of birds, primarily galliforms, during the growth period have been summarized by Scott (1973), Fisher (1972), and various authors in Bell and Freeman (1971). Requirements usually are determined either by measuring the rate of accumulation of a substance by the growing chick or by providing diets adequate for "normal" growth with the exception of one substance whose amount is varied. Other than the fact that the second method is based on experimentation, its advantages are that requirements can be determined for substances that are turned over rapidly rather than accumulated and that substances that can be synthesized by the chick are shown not to be essential requirements even though they are accumulated. Results of an experiment testing the growth performance of chicks on varied levels of sulfur amino acids (cystine and methionine) by Boomgardt and Baker (1973), are illustrated in Table III. In their study, weight gain and protein retention level off between dietary levels of sulfur amino acids of between 3.8 and 4.5% of crude protein. Lower dietary levels severely retarded growth.

The nutritional requirements of birds include 13 essential amino acids and adequate nitrogen for synthesis of nonessential amino acids (Boorman and Lewis, 1971), 13 essential inorganic elements (Butler, 1971), 13 vitamins (Coates, 1971), linoleic or arachidonic fatty acids, used to make prostaglandins (Horton, 1971), α-linolenic acid (Annison, 1971), and an adequate sup-

TABLE III

Growth Performance of Male Crossbred Chicks on Diets with Different Levels of Sulfur Amino Acids[a,b,c]

Growth performance	Sulfur amino acids (% crude protein)				
	1.7	2.4	3.1	3.8	4.5
Mass increase (g day^{-1})	1.4	4.2	9.2	14.4	15.7
Gain/feed (g g^{-1})	0.16	0.33	0.46	0.56	0.62
Protein retention (g day^{-1})	1.5	7.4	19.4	31.0	33.3
Energy retention (kcal day^{-1})	76	146	236	354	415

[a] Metabolizable energy of diet was 3000 kcal kg^{-1}.
[b] Age 8–21 days.
[c] After Boomgardt and Baker (1973).

ply of energy. As an energy source for growing chicks, carbohyrates can be completely replaced by protein and by triglycerides, but not by fatty acids alone, suggesting that certain carbohydrates may be essential requirements (Pearce and Brown, 1971). Dietary levels of most of these substances required by growing chicks were listed for the chicken by Scott et al. (1969) and for pheasants, quail, ducks, and turkeys by Scott (1973). These may not, however, be indicative of dietary requirements of other species, particularly for substances accumulated during growth, owing to differences in growth rate and body proportions. More rapidly growing birds may require greater concentrations of essential amino acids in the diet. Species with heavier plumages, such as many seabirds, may require higher concentrations of sulfur amino acids to support feather growth.

Potential nutritional limitations to growth rate might be identified by considering the composition of the foods of chicks. The amount of metabolizable energy per gram of food depends on the water and lipid contents and the indigestible fraction (Ricklefs 1974, p. 157). The ratios of metabolizable energy to ingested energy for different types of diets are, approximately: fish, 80%; insects, 60–70%; grains, 70–80%; and pine needles, willow buds, *Vaccinium* fruits, 30–40% for ptarmigan (Dunn, 1973; Kendeigh et al., 1977). Based on wet weight, grains contain high levels, and marine invertebrates, low levels, of metabolizable energy.

The ratio of protein (% dry weight) to metabolizable energy (kcal g^{-1}) varies from about 1 for tropical fruits, and 3 for grains to between 14 and 22 for animal foods depending on amounts of fat; pure protein has a ratio of 23 (Ricklefs, 1974). Among fruits, which provide the least protein, there is considerable variation which allows for the possibility of diet selection based on protein content. Summarizing the data of F. H. J. Crome on Australian fruits, Foster (1978) reported protein/energy ratios from considerably less than 1 to as high as 6 (*Ficus*, Moraceae). White (1974) reported high values of 4 (*Phytolacca*, Phytolaccaceae, and *Faramea*, Rubiaceae) and almost 6 (*Cordia*, Boraginaceae). Four species of *Ficus* varied between 1 and 2. Based on measurements of protein accumulation and oxygen consumption during the early part of the nestling period, White (1974) determined that Clay-colored Robins (*Turdus grayi*) and Yellow-bellied Elaenias (*Elaenia flavogaster*) required protein–energy ratios of between 6 and 9; hence fruits do not appear to provide adequate protein for rapid growth. The alternatives for tropical fruit-eating birds appear to be to supplement the diets of small nestlings with insects or to slow the rate of growth (Morton, 1973; Ricklefs, 1976; Foster, 1978). Relatively few tropical species feed their young exclusively fruit. Those that do, such as the Bearded Bellbird and Oilbird, grow about one-half as rapidly as other tropical species of similar body size (Ricklefs, 1976).

Grains are also rather deficient compared to the needs of rapidly growing chicks. For example, Street (1978) found that Mallard (*Anas platyrhynchos*) ducklings between ages 1 and 14 days fed on a seed (barley meal) diet (13.5% protein) increased their mass only 1.6-fold compared to 9.3-fold on an invertebrate diet (51.8% protein). Many species of seed eaters eat insects and other animal foods during the growth period. Doves provide their chicks with a secretion of the crop ("crop milk") during the early part of the nestling period (Vandeputte-Poma, 1980). Crop milk removed from chicks contains 48% protein by dry weight (Vandeputte-Poma, 1968) compared to 12% on average for grains.

The amino acid composition of most plant foods does not closely match the requirements of chicks, although combinations of grains can provide a well-balanced diet. Foster (1978) analyzed the amino acid contents of four species of tropical fruits and found that they were uniformly deficient in the essential amino acids histidine, methionine, and phenylalanine. Even animal foods may be deficient in quantitites of some amino acids under some circumstances. Several authors have suggested that sulfur amino acids may be limiting during periods of feather growth. Feathers contain 7–8% cysteine; foods such as fish flesh and liver contain only 3% methionine, which is interconvertible with cysteine. Amino acid deficiency does not seem likely among fish eaters, therefore, but may be a problem for frugivores and granivores.

Among mineral elements, most concern for potential growth limitation has focused on calcium, which is necessary for bone development. Although species that feed on prey having bones or calcareous shells are probably not limited by calcium availability, others are. Houston (1978) suggested that griffon vultures (*Gyps* sp.) may have a calcium deficiency because they eat only soft tissues of carcasses. Chicks of many species of passerines are fed fragments of teeth, bone, and eggshells to supplement their normal insect diets. Craneflies and sawflies are about 0.1% calcium by dry weight, which is not sufficient for bone growth in Lapland Longspurs (*Calcarius lapponicus*; Seastedt and MacLean, 1977). Nestlings older than 3 days are fed the teeth and bones of lemmings, and the 0.55% calcium in their feces indicates that the supplement may be more than adequate.

Scott (1973) indicated that galliform chicks require about 20–30 mg calcium per gram of protein in their diet. The 0.1% calcium by dry weight of some insects is probably equivalent to 10–20 mg per gram protein. Fruits appear to be extremely variable, ranging from less than 1 mg g^{-1} (*Rourea*, Connaraceae) to 50 (*Eugenia*, *Virola*) and 177 (*Miconia*) mg g^{-1} (White, 1974).

The foregoing data emphasize how poorly we understand the nutrition of chicks under natural conditions. The data on requirements of poultry are extensive but cannot be taken as the standard for all birds. The nutritional values of natural foods, particularly the contents of amino acids, trace elements, and vitamins, are virtually unknown. The search for nutritionally limiting diets should start with slowly growing species, which will be identified in Sections IX,A and IX,B,4.

V. Mathematical Description of Growth

A. Purpose of Description

The data of growth are measurements of size in a sample of individuals or a single individual over time. Growth data are usually collected in much greater detail than one can easily use to compare growth processes among populations or other samples. Hence, they must be distilled to a level that matches the process of concern. If one is interested in whether population A grows more rapidly than population B, one has to adopt a single measure that is a meaningful expression of *growth rate*. It may be the time from hatching to fledging, the number of doublings in size during the first week after hatching, or the number of days required to accomplish a certain amount of growth. Using such simple indices may lead to unrealistic assumptions about the nature of the growth process and, in turn, to unjustified conclusions. More complex descriptions of growth may be difficult to compare meaningfully, particularly when many correlated parameters, such as sizes at various ages, are involved. The most straightforward approach to the description of growth is to fit the data of growth to models with a few interpretable parameters. The number of parameters depends on the complexity of the growth function. Two (intercept or initial size and slope or rate of increase) are needed to describe linear increase. Three are needed for sigmoid curves (initial size, rate, and final size or asymptote). Four parameters are needed in sigmoid curve fitting if the shape of the curve is to be a variable.

Curve fitting serves two purposes. It simplifies the data of growth by extracting a few variables that adequately describe the course of growth over time or of the relative growth of two or more components. It also resolves data on size versus time or size versus size into components of growth dynamics that can provide the basis for analysis and interpretation.

B. Types of Data

The most common types of growth data are dimensions and masses of individuals and their parts, although measurements of behavior and physiol-

TABLE IV

Classification of the Types of Growth Data[a]

Age of individuals	Number of records per individual		
	One	Few[b]	Complete
Uniform	Static (S)	—[c]	—
Variable and known	Cross-sectional (CS)	Mixed longitudinal (ML)	Longitudinal (L)
Variable and unknown	Mixed cross-sectional (MC)	Interval (I)	—

[a] After Cock (1966).
[b] As few as two but not so many as to provide a complete description of growth for any one individual.
[c] A dash signifies that categories are not logically possible.

ogy could also be considered as basic data of growth. The most common external measurements of birds are described by Baldwin *et al.* (1931), which should be referred to explicitly in describing measurements for the sake of uniformity in comparison. Measurements of mass are likely to vary with time of day and time since last feeding. These sources of variability should be acknowledged.

Samples of data from a population vary in their application depending upon whether individuals are measured once, several times, or at regular intervals throughout the growth period and whether the ages that accompany each record of measurements are uniform or variable and, if variable, known or unknown. The different types of data classified by these criteria are summarized in Table IV. Clearly longitudinal (L) data are the most comprehensive and useful, followed by mixed longitudinal (ML), cross-sectional (CS) or interval (I), and mixed cross-sectional (MC) or static data, depending on the purpose of the analysis.

C. Types of Analyses

Static data, of which records are measurements repeated over individuals of the same age, can be used for comparisons among subsamples or populations and for analyzing relationships among measurements within age groups. Usually the age at measurement corresponds to a major stage or event in the life cycle, such as hatching, fledging, or adulthood, but one might also choose an arbitrary age for comparison, for example of mass at age 10 days, or substitute some physiological or anatomical state for age, as in comparisons of peak nestling mass. Analysis of relationships among variables within age classes might involve bivariate comparisons, such as determining allometric constants from log–log plots, or a multivariate analysis, such as determining the eigenvectors of a correlation or covariance matrix (e.g., principal components analysis). Such analyses can be accomplished with all types of data, but considerations of sample size may favor the taking of static data rather than a more time-consuming type of data.

A frequent type of analysis is to fit an equation to the time course of growth in order to derive a few descriptive variables of the complete growth curve. The variables may then be compared among samples in much the same manner as are static data. Curve fitting of this type can be done only with CS-, ML-, and L-type data, although it is possible to derive estimated ages from I data, thereby converting it to ML data for some purposes (Ricklefs and White, 1975). As explained later (Section V,D,4), statistical comparisons between samples are different for derived growth variables based on CS data versus ML and L data.

Analysis of the relative growth of parts or components of organisms, including the relationship between size and shape during growth, can be accomplished with data for individuals of unknown age, and therefore is applicable to MC and I data as well as CS, ML, and L data. If the objectives of the study include analysis of variation among individuals within a population, the data must be at least ML or I.

Investigators frequently wish to know if the value for a variable at a particular age is predictive of or predicted by the value of the same variable at a different age or some other variable at a different age for the same individual. Such analyses usually involve correlation and regression, for ex-

TABLE V

APPLICABILITY OF ANALYSES TO THE TYPES OF DATA ON GROWTH

Types of analysis	Type of data[a]					
	MC	S	I	CS	ML[b]	L
Comparison of means		x	x	x	x	x
Relationships among variables						
Within age classes		x	x	x	x	x
Over age classes	x		x	x	x	x
Curve-fitting to time course of growth			(x)[c]	x	x	x
Longitudinal correlations and cross-correlations					x	x

[a]MC, Mixed cross-sectional; S, static; I, interval; CS, cross-sectional; ML, mixed longitudinal; L, longitudinal.

[b]Value of mixed longitudinal data for most analyses improves with number and regularity of observations.

[c]Can be used for fitting equations in which initial age is arbitrary.

ample of neonate weight versus egg size (e.g., Ricklefs et al., 1978) or of weight at age x versus neonate weight (e.g., O'Connor, 1975b). For this type of analysis, only ML and L data are suitable, although comparisons can also be made between a very small number of static samples of measurements of the same individuals (e.g., at hatching and adulthood), and age may be replaced by some arbitrary development scale such as time at fledging, depending on the purpose of the analysis.

Comprehensive multivariate analyses of longitudinal data have been attempted for data on birds only by O'Connor (1978b). The applicability of these analyses to the various types of data is summarized in Table V.

D. Curve Fitting

The objective of curve fitting is to use an equation having few variables to describe the time course of longitudinal data. The description generally improves with the number of variables in the equation but because simplification of the data is desired, one must choose an equation that provides an adequate or useful, rather than complete, description. Curvefitting may be based on CS, ML, L, and in some applications I data. L and, to a lesser extent, ML data allow one to assess variation among individuals; CS data restrict analyses to variation between samples. The notation in this section will be based on analysis of masses (M) or lengths (L) as a function of age (x) or, in the case of interval data, time (t). Thus $M(x)$ is the mass at age x. For convention, the age at hatching is designated 0 and that of the adult, ∞. For interval data $M(t)$ and $M(t+i)$ are the masses at the beginning and end of interval i.

1. Growth Models

Ricker (1979) and Pruitt et al. (1979) have provided comprehensive reviews of growth models and their derivations. Most growth equations, especially those in early use, were developed to model biological processes that underlie growth. Derivations usually start with a consideration of growth rate dM/dt as some function of the mass achieved, hence

$$dM/dt = f(M) \tag{1}$$

The simplest expressions for f are $f(M) = a$, which describes linear growth at rate a (absolute increase per unit time), and $f(M) = aM$, which describes exponential growth. Although equations of the type $M(t) = a + bt$ and $M(t) = a \exp(bt)$ have been used to describe segments of growth curves, both increase continuously with time and therefore neither provides an adequate description of asymptotic growth.

Asymptotic growth equations share the common property that $f(M)$ decreases to zero, as M approaches the final weight plateau or asymptote. Such functions usually have two terms; one expresses a tendency of the organism to grow and the other expresses factors that restrict growth, hence

$$dM/dt = f(M) - g(M) \tag{2}$$

The logistic equation (Robertson, 1908) may be expressed as

$$dM/dt = aM - bM^2 \tag{3}$$

where a is the exponential tendency of mass to increase and b is the rate at which this tendency is restricted or damped as mass increases. According to the logistic equation, growth continues until $a = bM$, hence the asymptote of the growth equation $M(\infty)$ is equal to a/b. Equation (3) can be reexpressed as the differential equation

$$dM/dt = aM \left[\frac{M(\infty) - M}{M(\infty)} \right] \tag{4}$$

which can now be integrated to give

$$M(t) = M(\infty)/(1 + e^{-Kt}) \tag{5}$$

which describes increase over time. The constant a has been replaced by the more familiar K, and time t is measured backward and forward from age at the inflection point of the growth curve $\frac{1}{2}M(\infty)$. When the time scale is shifted such that 0 is the age at hatching, Eq. (5) becomes

$$M(x) = \frac{M(\infty)}{1 + \left[\frac{M(\infty) - M(0)}{M(0)} \right] e^{-Kx}} \tag{6}$$

The logistic equation describes a sigmoid curve with a fixed form (see Ricklefs 1967a, 1968b), where the specific growth rate decreases in direct proportion to the fraction of the asymptote achieved [Eq. (4)]. The growth model has three parameters: $M(\infty)$, the asymptotic measurement usually in units of mass or length; $M(0)$ the initial size, usually measured at hatching; and K, the rate constant of the equation whose units are 1/time. As explained later, fitting the logistic equation to longitudinal or cross-sectional data yields estimates of the parameters $M(\infty)$, $M(0)$, and K, which can be used for comparisons between samples or populations (see Section V,D,4).

Several other equations that describe sigmoid curves with different shapes have found frequent application to data on birds. The Gompertz equation (Gompertz, 1825; Laird et al., 1965) is based on the function

$$dM/dt = KM[\log M(\infty) - \log M] \qquad (7)$$

in which the specific growth rate decreases in proportion to the logarithm of the mass attained. Although the Gompertz equation has the difficult property that dM/Mdt approaches minus infinity as M approaches zero, it has been found to describe the postnatal growth of many species of birds adequately. The integrated form of the equation is

$$M(x) = M(\infty) \exp\{-[\log M(\infty) - \log M(0)] \exp(-Kx)\} \qquad (8)$$

A third three-parameter equation in common use is the Pütter (1920) equation, also named for von Bertalanffy (1938, 1957), who elaborated its applications. The Pütter or von Bertalanffy equation is based on a generalized expression of the form

$$dM/dt = aM^m - bM^n \qquad (9)$$

Von Bertalanffy suggested that the term for increase is proportional to surface area and that for decrease is proportional to mass M. Although his reasoning has no particular biological basis, the resulting equation

$$dM/dt = aM^{2/3} - bM \qquad (10)$$

has been shown to agree closely with the growth curves of some species of birds (Ricklefs, 1968b) and many other organisms. The integrated form of Eq. (10) is

$$M(x) = M(\infty) \left\{ 1 - \left[\frac{M(\infty)^{1/3} - M(0)^{1/3}}{M(0)^{1/3}} \right] \exp(-Kx) \right\}^3 \qquad (11)$$

The shapes of the three sigmoid equations described earlier are shown in Fig. 3, in which each has identical values of $M(0)$ and absolute rate of growth (dM/dt) at the inflection point. The von Bertalanffy curve attains its maximum rate of growth earlier than the Gompertz and logistic curves and at a lower fraction of the asymptote, $\frac{8}{27}M(\infty)$ [0.296 $M(\infty)$] versus $M(\infty)/e$

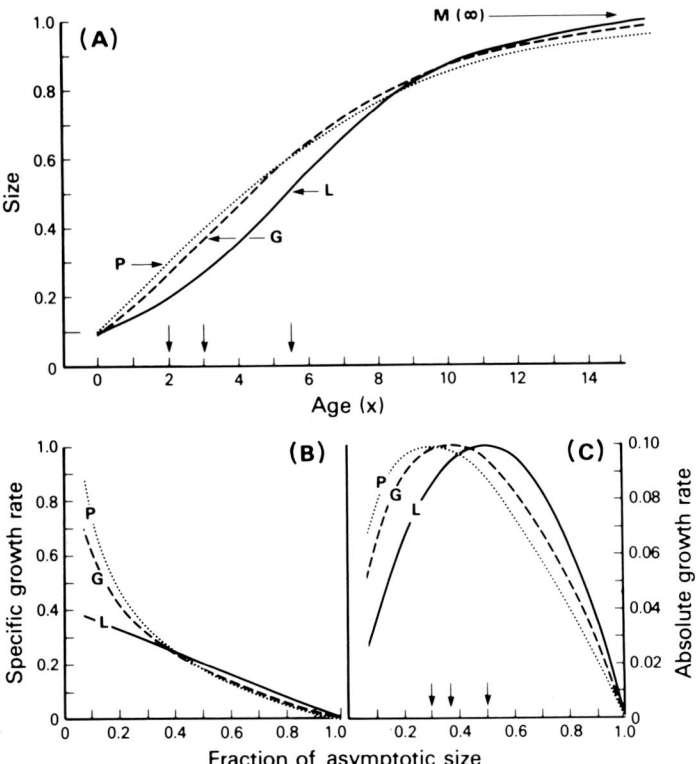

FIG. 3. Comparison of cumulative increase (A), specific growth rate (B), and absolute growth rate (C) for Pütter or von Bertalanffy (P), Gompertz (G), and logistic (L) equations having identical values of $M(0)$ (0.10) and $dM(I)/dt$ (0.10). Inflection points and ages at inflection (I) are indicated by arrows.

$[0.368M(\infty)]$ and $\frac{1}{2}M(\infty)$ $[0.500\ M(\infty)]$. Conversely, the approach to the asymptote is prolonged in the von Bertalanffy curve compared to the Gompertz and, especially, logistic curves.

The idea that lengths are proportional to mass as the power of $\frac{1}{3}$ provided the stimulus for a second form of Pütter's equation

$$L(x) = L(\infty)\left\{ 1 - \left[\frac{L(\infty) - L(0)}{L(0)}\right]\exp(-Kx) \right\} \quad (12)$$

which has found wide application to the description of length increase and was used by Brody (1937, 1945) to describe postinflection portions of curves of mass increase of animals. Equation (12) differs from sigmoid curves in that it has no inflection point.

Three-parameter sigmoid equations have a fixed shape and vary only in asymptote, growth rate, and initial size or, alternatively, a constant that relates time to age. Several authors have introduced equations with a fourth parameter for the shape of the growth curve. The most successful of these is the Richards equation (Richards, 1959; White and Ratti, 1977), which is based on the following version of the differential [Eq. (9)],

$$dM/dt = \pm aM^m \pm bM \qquad (13)$$

(the signs of a and b depend on whether $m < 1$ or $m > 1$). One integrated form of the Richards equation is

$$M(x) = \{M(\infty)^{1-m} - [M(\infty)^{1-m} - M(0)^{1-m}]\exp[-(1-m)Kx]\}^{1/(1-m)} \qquad (14)$$

which resembles the Pütter equation, as one might expect. The Richards equation is a generalized sigmoid equation with shape controlled by parameter m such that the von Bertalanffy equation is the special case of $m = \frac{2}{3}$ and the logistic equation is that of $m = 2$. The limit of the Richards equation as m approaches 1 [and $1/(1-m)$ approaches infinity] is the Gompertz equation.

The above equations are expressed in terms of parameters $M(\infty)$, $M(0)$, K, and m, but they may be written in terms of combinations of these four. In one frequent expression $M(0)$ is replaced by mass at the inflection point $M(I)$ and age x by $(t - I)$ or $(x - I)$, where I is the time or age at the inflection point. For the logistic model, because $M(I) = \frac{1}{2}M(\infty)$, $[M(\infty) - M(I)]/M(I) = 1$ and Eq. (6) may be written

$$M(t) = M(\infty)\{1 + \exp[-K(t - I)]\}^{-1} \qquad (15)$$

2. Transformed Time Scales

Brody (1937) used an equation similar to Eq. (12) to derive a "physiologic" time scale on which curves having different values of K are made to coincide. The values of the physiologic time scale are $K(t - I)$, and therefore it is dimensionless. Ricklefs (1967a) proposed a similar time scale of growth units, each of which was the period required to increase from 10 to 50% of asymptotic size. The major application of such transformed time scales is to compare developmental changes independently of the increase in mass or length of a particular appendage. Ricklefs and Hainsworth (1968) compared the development of homeothermy in several passerines in this way, and Ricklefs (1973, 1979a) has used the scale to compare stage of growth at fledging and the development of body organs and appendages among birds with very different growth rates (see Fig. 2).

3. Fitting Growth Models

Linear models may be fitted to data by linear regression, as may exponential models after log transformation of the size data. Sigmoid models are more difficult to fit to data because they normally require complicated transformations to linearize data or computerized nonlinear fitting techniques.

A preliminary step is to determine whether all the parameters of the equation need be treated as variables. When it is possible to measure initial size and asymptote directly, these parameters may be fixed, leaving only growth rate and, if the Richards equation is used, shape to be fitted to the data.

Various transformations to linearize data are discussed by Nair (1954). An additional transformation discussed by Ricklefs (1967a) illustrates the technique for the logistic equation. By rearranging Eq. (6), we obtain

$$\log\left[\frac{M(t)}{M(\infty) - M(t)}\right] = Kt - KI \tag{16}$$

Hence if masses are transformed as the left-hand term in the equation, the parameters K and I can be estimated by linear regression, $y = a + bx$, where $K = b$ and $I = -a/K$. Notice that if the value of $M(\infty)$ is not fixed, it must be estimated by trial and error. In addition to this problem, values of M greater than $M(\infty)$ are not admissible because the left-hand term in brackets is then negative, and the transformed values do not meet the conditions for linear regression. In particular, the residuals of $\log\{M(t)/[M(\infty)-M(t)]\}$ become very large as $M(t)$ approaches either 0 or $M(\infty)$. These and other problems are discussed at length by Nair (1954).

Although transformation has been used extensively to fit equations to growth curves and in practice yields reasonable estimates for three-parameter equations, the preferred method of curve fitting is by nonlinear least squares (NLIN) estimation. Computer programs for application of this technique are available as a part of most statistical packages, such as SAS, BMDP, and SPSS. NLIN techniques use progressive iteration to find the combination of values for parameters that minimize the squared deviations of data from the model. Considering the wide availability of computers, NLIN techniques should replace regression based on transformation, including my graphical approach (Ricklefs, 1967a). I have found that comparisons between the techniques are generally favorable, but NLIN holds greater promise for statistical comparison of data, as discussed later.

A practical difficulty of NLIN estimation is that some of the parameters are not linear with respect to each other: rather, they enter the growth models as various products and quotients, $M(0) \exp(-K)$ being a frequent one. As a result, parameters are likely to be highly correlated close to the point of the